GET BACK UP
The Billy Taylor Story

GET BACK UP
The Billy Taylor Story

Billy Taylor

To Thorn,

Thanks for remembering
me over the years — I ap-
preciate your support.
Your friend
Billy Taylor
#42

1/19/06

By
Dr. Billy Taylor
And Kevin Allen

Foreword by: Bo Schembechler

Touchdown Billy Taylor
Bob Ufer, Voice of Michigan Football for 5 decades
www.ufer.org

Published by
Immortal Investments Publishing
www.immortalinvestemtns.com
35122 W. Michigan Avenue, Wayne, Michigan 48184
1-800-475-2066

First Edition
August, 2005
ISBN: 0-9723637-7-7

**Publisher's Cataloging-In-Publication Data
(Prepared by The Donohue Group, Inc.)**

Taylor, Billy, 1949-
  Get back up : the Billy Taylor story / Billy Taylor & Kevin M. Allen ; foreword by Bo Schembechler.-- 1st ed.

    p. ; cm.
  ISBN: 0-9723637-7-7

1. Taylor, Billy, 1949- 2. Alcoholics--Rehabilitation. 3. Narcotic addicts--Rehabilitation. 4. Recovering alcoholics--Biography. 5. Football players--Biography. 6. Spiritual healing. I. Allen, Kevin M. II. Title.

GV939.T39 T39 2005
796.332/092/4 B   2005930016

"Experience is not what happens to you, it is what you do with what happens to you."

—Aldous Huxley

To the memory of my mother Mariah Marie Taylor and my father William L. Taylor, Sr. To my children Mariah, Alden, William III, Lewis and to all the members of their generation who may experience many of the same choices, challenges, opportunities and achievements.

—Dr. Billy Taylor
Get Back Up

CONTENTS

FOREWORD

Bo Schembechler

Former Football Coach

University of Michigan

WHAT MANY PEOPLE DON'T REALIZE IS THAT Billy Taylor wasn't necessarily destined to carry the ball on the "Touchdown Billy Taylor, Touchdown Billy Taylor" play against Ohio State in 1971. That wasn't the play that we called on the sidelines. But before the game, we had instructed our quarterbacks that if Ohio State was in man-to-man coverage it meant they were going to come after us. Our back-up quarterback, Larry Cipa, was in the game. When he walked up to the line of scrimmage, he read that defensive coverage and knew what he was supposed to do. He checked into that option pitch to Billy. He knew that everyone would be caught inside. They would have no support on the outside because the linebackers were committed.

Once Cipa made the read, called the down-the-line option and executed the pitch, Billy could do the rest.

Billy had great vision as a back. He could anticipate and envision what was likely going to occur before the play actually unfolded. He had the ability to make quick, shallow cuts. The quickness of his cuts would leave defenders off balance. And they couldn't tackle Billy unless they could get their body into him. Billy had strong, powerful legs and he would run right through arm tackles.

He had good speed, not great speed. He had good hands, not great hands. He was an average blocker. But when you handed him the football, he had a knack of being able to read the defense and use his strength to power through there. He was a darn good back.

We took advantage of what he could do. Although many of Billy's plays running out of the "I Formation" looked the same, they were actually all quite different. We always varied our blocking schemes to confuse the defense. We didn't base block all the time. We would block down or trap or use other combinations. We would make it challenging for the defense by coming at them from all angles. It was the running back's job to interpret what was happening.

Billy had to know how the play was going to be blocked, because the defenders react differently to every blocking combination. That was one of his strengths. He was creative enough to understand how a series of blocks was going to create the room he needed to run. When the ball was in his hands, he knew what to do with it. He had a gift.

Actually, I didn't recruit Billy to come to Michigan. I was at Miami when he was at Barberton High School, and I tried to convince him to come to Miami. I tried to persuade all of those Ohio players to come to Miami including Thom Darden and Dan Dierdorf. When I arrived at Michigan, I already knew what I had.

Billy and I were both from Barberton, Ohio and maybe there was an instant connection there. My mother still lived in Barberton when Billy played there, and I think Billy even had supper at my mother's house.

Before Billy and the Mellow Men came to Michigan, there were only a few black players on the Wolverines' squad. They were already here when I came to Michigan, and I'm not shy about saying the reason I won right away was that I inherited some good football players. There was no magic coaching. Billy Taylor was a good player. Reggie McKenzie was a good player. Glenn Doughty was a magnificent athlete. Butch Carpenter was a good football player. Mike Taylor was a good football player. Mike Oldham made some contributions. These black athletes made a difference.

I was shocked when I heard that Billy was connected to a bank robbery. I won't lie to you. I was very disappointed in him. But I never considered abandoning him. Billy and I had some differences, but they were always minor. He was never in any significant trouble. He didn't strike me as the kind of person who would be involved in a major crime.

As much as I appreciate what Billy has to say about my contributions to his life, I don't believe I was any kind of savior. I just did what I believed needed to be done to help one of my players. That's part of what the Michigan football program is about. We've always tried to take care of our players when they needed assistance and support. I've always wanted my players to know that I was still behind them even after their career was over. Even when Billy was sentenced to prison, we didn't give up on him.

Actually, I have a great deal of respect for Billy for earning his master's degree while he was in prison. It would have been easy for him to surrender his dreams and educational ambitions when he found himself in trouble. Even today, he still continues to pursue higher degrees of education.

Billy has said that Michigan taught him perseverance. Maybe The Billy Taylor Story illustrates that aspect of Michigan tradition. We don't give up on each other and we don't give up on ourselves. If you are a Michigan man, there is no quit in you.

—Bo Schembechler

DR. BILLY TAYLOR TRIBUTE

Jim Brandstatter

Teammate of Billy Taylor 1969-1971

University of Michigan

THE LESSONS WE LEARNED AS FOOTBALL PLAYERS growing up together at the University of Michigan in the late 60's and early 70's are lessons that stayed with us throughout life. Billy Taylor had to put those lessons to work after graduation far more than most of us, and his book "Get Back Up" is a classic tale of overcoming adversity through hard work and faith.

As a player Billy was as good as they get. Named All-American after his senior year at Michigan, life was full of promise and dreams fulfilled. However, life threw Billy a curveball, and a bad decision made all of the dreams and hard work crumble around him.

From the top of the world to the bottom is a long journey, but it doesn't take long. Billy took the journey, but he didn't let the fall defeat him. Just as we learned on the practice fields in Ann Arbor getting ready to play for the Wolverines, no matter how bad the situation looked, you never gave up. You never stopped fighting.

Billy Taylor's story is about a young man who never gave up, and never stopped fighting to regain his good name. He didn't let a mistake define him rather; he used the mistake as motivation to re-define his life. It wasn't an easy road, but nothing good ever comes easily.

Billy Taylor's story is an inspiration to anyone who thinks they don't have a chance. It's the story of triumph against the odds. It's a story of perseverance in the face of fear and self doubt. It's the story of never giving up. It's the story of getting back up after a fall. It's a story we can all learn from, and take with us as we continue with our own lives.

—Jim Brandstatter

ACKNOWLEDGEMENTS

By Dr. Billy Taylor

GET BACK UP IS A PERSONAL JOURNEY, but its publication could not have been possible without the support, inspiration and assistance from many members of my family, friends, teammates, coaches, mentors, professors, and professional associates.

I first must acknowledge my parents, Mr. William L.Taylor, Sr., and Mrs. Mariah Marie Taylor, who are no longer with us. Mom and Dad, I love you. I also acknowledge my children, William L. Taylor III, Alden James Taylor, Mariah Marie Taylor and their mother, Cheryl Marie Taylor; and my son Lewis LaMont Askew. All of you have been and are an important part of my life. My sisters, Lucille, Clara and Juanita and my brothers Jim, Felix and my late brother Thomas (Jack). Your support during my childhood, my achievements and my failures has given me strength to persevere.

Wolverine coach Bo Schembechler, UNLV Doctoral Advisor Dr. Paul Meacham, University of Michigan academic mentor, Dr. Charles Moody and wife Christella, have instilled in me the discipline it takes to achieve on the field, in the classroom and in life. The lessons I have learned from them have set the stage for my life's achievements and reinforced the importance of setting high goals and working hard to attain them.

A very special and thankful acknowledgement of my mother Mariah Marie Taylor who gave me life and taught me to love God, be prayerful and have faith. My sister Sheryl Carson who believed in me when I needed someone to say, "You can do it!"

I must thank many, many more people, too numerous to name individually, who encouraged me; who believed, as I did, that this book will help others to overcome equally difficult circumstances in their lives. Thanks to Ned Gershenson (Farrah, Jeremy and Jorden) for encouraging me to write my story. And a sincere appreciation to Kevin Allen, Jennifer Hilliker, Michael Reddy and Karen Saslaw for assisting me in remembering events, finding photos, checking dates and facts and attending to the technical and business aspects of writing and publishing *Get Back Up.*

Finally, without the intervention, direction and blessing of my Lord Jesus Christ, I would not be sharing this life story and its lessons with you today. Thank you Lord.

—Dr. Billy Taylor

INTRODUCTION

By Dr. Billy Taylor

NO PERSON CAN RELIVE THE BEST MOMENT of his or her life, but at least mine is available on DVD and audiocassette. My 30 seconds of pure uncut joy and extra-strength exhilaration came as time was evaporating during the Michigan vs. Ohio State football game on November 21, 1971.

My Wolverines were trailing 6-3 with just over two minutes remaining. On a third-and-long play deep in Ohio State territory, Coach Bo Schembechler opted to put the ball into my hands.

When the football was pitched to me on a sweep, it seemed as if we were all moving in slow motion. I could see our linemen pulling and moving as efficiently and gracefully as the best Broadway choreography. Bo Rather made a crack-back block and I saw an opponent flipping in front of me. Fullback Fritz Seyferth was like a bulldozer in front of me as we turned the corner. There were about four Buckeyes in our path to the end zone. One by one, each Ohio State defender was toppled. The Michigan blocking was devastating. There was one defender with a true shot at me but Fritz erased him like he had never been there. Another Buckeye came out of nowhere but I out-ran him. I waltzed into the end zone untouched for the winning score. That gave us an undefeated regular season and a Rose Bowl invitation.

On my desk today is a bobblehead portrayal of the famed Michigan radio broadcaster Bob Ufer. When you press a button, you hear his lyrical, passionate description of that play:

"Billy Taylor is down to the 20, down to 15, down to 10, 5, 4, 3, 2, 1. Touchdown Billy Taylor, Touchdown Billy Taylor. Billy Taylor scores a touchdown from 21 yards out. The crowd is going berserk."

It is considered one of the more dramatic moments in Michigan football history. It was a moment that young players dream of experiencing. It was almost a perfect moment for an athlete. It was my moment.

At that precise moment I reached the endzone and raised my arms to the heavens, my life seemed perfect. I was a three-time All-American tailback for the University of Michigan. I was, and still am today, the only running back in Michigan history to average 100 yards per game. I was soon to be a Michigan graduate with a degree in education. I was a Christian whose faith in God was unwavering. I had a sweet, dear mother who had raised me by herself, working six days a week in a laundry to make sure there was supper on the table and moral values in the home. I had a bushel of friends, including a handful of proud African American men like Reggie McKenzie, Thom Darden, Glenn Doughty, Mike Taylor, Butch Carpenter and Mike Oldham who lived with me in a house on Geddes Road that we called the Den of the Mellow Men.

The National Football League was on the horizon. I had patterned my running style after the legendary Jim Brown and I was being told I could be selected as high as the second round in the NFL draft. There was no doubt in my mind I was going to be a 1,000-yard NFL rusher. I was driven to succeed. I had lightning in my legs and poetry in my soul. When my NFL career was over, I planned to be an educator and writer. I thought I had much to give, and plenty of time to give it.

If I could have been interviewed seconds after crossing the goal line against Ohio State, I would have sworn to you that I was destined for a life of success and grandeur.

At that moment, you could not have convinced me that four years later I would be a convicted felon, serving time in a federal penitentiary for being a co-conspirator in a bank robbery in my hometown of Barberton, Ohio.

No one who knew me well at the time of that Ohio State game would have believed that I was destined to become a drug and alcohol addict in the 1980s, drifting from odd job to odd job. None of my friends would have believed that by the 1990s I would be homeless on the streets of Detroit, reduced to doing whatever I had to support my habit.

I owned a master's degree from the University of Michigan, and yet one night I severely cut my hand trying to help another addict break into a pay phone to extract enough coins to purchase a pint of liquor.

Instead of writing poetry and educating the youth of America, I was standing on the street corner with pimps and whores shouting obscenities at police officers. I no longer associated with good men like McKenzie, Darden and others. I hung out with people who had labels and descriptions instead of names—Skinny Jim, Hawkface and Whiskey John. My best friend those days was a hooker named Little Bit, a petite young women from a good home whose drug habit was as consuming as my own. No one on the streets had any idea that I was Billy Taylor, the former All-American running back. To them, I was just "Bill." I was just another addict, no more, no less. I was just like them, always scheming to scrounge up $2.10 for a pint of vodka or $5 for the cheapest 12-pack or $15 for a bag of weed.

During my days on the streets, I must have been arrested 20 times on a variety of misdemeanor offenses and sometimes I got a few days of jail time, complete with a warm bed and some occasional food, so it was worth the aggravation. On cold winter's nights, when you are lying on the floor of a vacant home wrapped in seven layers of smelly clothes trying not to freeze to death, the county jail seems like a Marriott Hotel.

It would take a battery of psychologists to properly explain how an educated man with lofty goals had reached a point that he could wear everything he owned.

However, today I have a better understanding of my descent into the dark side, and I can describe the miracle that brought me back to life. It was truly a miracle.

It was just before daybreak, maybe around 5:00 in the morning on August 17, 1997, and I was sitting in front of an abandoned building behind the liquor store on Lakewood with several cans of Black Label and a fifth of Mohawk. I had walked most of the night in Detroit, hanging out on the corners, talking about everything and nothing with anyone who would listen. I had settled into my seat on the porch to finish off my liquor. By that time in my addiction, I had such a high tolerance of alcohol that I could finish a fifth and not be falling down drunk. I would be high, but functional. At that moment, I was thinking about what my first hustle of the day would be. I was already planning how I could earn money for my next round of alcohol.

When you are living on the streets, you develop a sense of perimeter security. I checked and re-checked to make sure I was by myself before I settled in. I was alone. I was sure of that.

That's why I was startled when a voice boomed: "William Taylor come forth."

It scared me so badly that I jumped up and dropped my vodka. When the bottle exploded on the cement, my anger erupted. I began to curse and yell and I was prepared to pound whoever had caused me to lose my drink. There was an alley separating the liquor store and the building, but no one was there. I looked through the high grass in front of the building and circled around it and reconfirmed I was very much alone.

When I returned to the front of the building, it occurred to me that the voice may not have been earthly. I began to shake. I was petrified. For the first time in years, I was not concerned about what I was drinking. I abandoned my beer and started double-timing toward Jefferson Avenue. For reasons I cannot explain, I walked right out in the middle of the road without concerning myself with traffic. Cars were coming in both directions, and yet they all missed me. It defies logic to explain why I was not struck.

The miracle that occurred over the next eight hours, and the journey that brought me to that place and time, is the story contained in these chapters. It's a story about the frailty of the human soul. It's the story about faith, the loss of faith and the restoration of faith. It's a story about the cruelty of drug addiction and the kindness of one woman who looked beyond matted hair, a dirty face and disheveled appearance to see a human being who could make a difference in the lives of others. It's a story about transforming nightmares into dreams of success. It's the story about how an athlete who found success on the football field by willing himself to get up after every hard tackle realized that he had to embrace the same attitude to conquer alcoholism. When you get knocked down, you have to "Get Back Up." That's what I did when I was Michigan's No. 1 tailback. That's what I did in 1997 when I was being slowly killed by my own addiction. I got back up because I realized I had more plays remaining in my life. I wanted more chances to find the end zone in other arenas of my life. This is the Billy Taylor story. I hope it helps you stay or get back up.

—*Dr. Billy Taylor*
Get Back Up

CHAPTER 1

BARBERTON, OHIO

THE MISTAKE THAT COACH WOODY HAYES made when he recruited me to Ohio State in 1968 was that his sales pitch was designed for the wrong target audience. Although I was a 1,000-yard rusher at Barberton High School, my 57-year-old mother Mariah Marie Taylor was the true recruit. What Woody didn't seem to grasp is that Momma was a devout Christian woman with serious reservations about the sport of football for spiritual and economic reasons.

Woody should have remembered that when Barberton coaches were forecasting greatness for Bill Taylor before my junior year in high school, Mariah Marie Taylor had stopped me right in my tracks. She wouldn't sign the permission slip necessary for me to play. Both she and my Aunt Ernestine Bibbs lived by the scriptures and couldn't quite reconcile football as being a Christian activity.

"Football is too worldly," Aunt Ernestine said. "Boys bet on football and where there is gambling there is sinning. We can't let this child get mixed up in football."

Momma was a single mom with seven children, struggling every day to keep food on the table and the electrical and gas bill paid. She worked at Sam Sing's laundry up to 10 hours per day and still every week she had to juggle our finances—"robbing Peter to pay Paul" as she would put it—to keep us a half-step ahead of the bill collectors. Food stamps, Goodwill Stores and utility shut-off were as much a part of our life as the Holy Bible. We were a poor black family just trying to survive. Momma's other objection about high school football was a practical concern.

"Child, you are going to get all broken up playing football and you will get out of high school and you won't be able to get yourself a good job," Momma said about denying me the opportunity to play football.

More than anything, Momma wanted a better life for me than she was living. That objective never changed, even though a year later she relented and allowed me to play my senior season for the Barberton Magics. "I saw how sad you were without football," Momma said. "But I will still worry that you will get all broken up."

"Don't worry Momma," I insisted, "I won't get hurt."

Now a few months after that conversation, I was an all-state football player with 57 scholarship offers. We still had bills and struggles, but suddenly we had hope, and a promise of a better life. "I just want one of my children to go to college and graduate," Momma often said.

Momma was excited that I was going to be able to attend college. But that didn't mean that she was going to abandon her religious beliefs. When Woody sat in our living room to tell us about the wonder of football in nearby Columbus, Ohio, he should have reminded himself to recruit Mariah Marie Taylor instead of Billy Taylor.

The problem was that Woody became animated when he talked about football. He was an excitable man who would sometimes forget that he wasn't always talking with the boys down at the garage. He would occasionally slip a cuss word into his conversation in the form of both nouns and adjectives.

"Damn Bill you should have been at practice yesterday," Woody said at one point. "Jack Tatum came up and knocked the hell out of the ball carrier three or four times."

Woody had used profanity in Momma's living room. I caught a glance from Momma. She was peeping over the top of her glasses. She was shaking her head in disbelief. At that moment, I knew I wasn't going to Ohio State. My mother and Aunt Ernestine were so strict in their faith that I was not even allowed to watch the NFL on Sunday in our home because my mom and aunt thought it would lead me down the path to betting and gambling. I had to go find another place to watch Jim Brown and the Cleveland Browns.

It was a major event in my school when Coach Hayes had come to visit earlier in the day. He was already a legend in Ohio by then. I remember his visit quite well, particularly because I had inadvertently made a poor fashion decision that day. I had just returned from a recruiting visit to Michigan and I was wearing a Michigan sweatshirt when Woody came to my school to get me. My French teacher was speechless. Here was Woody Hayes bigger than life in our classroom. Everyone in the room was gasping for air. She brought him back to my cubicle where I was sitting with my headphones on listening to French tapes. When Woody spotted my shirt he said, "We got to get you a real shirt."

My mom and I still went out with Woody to the Brown Derby for dinner. He was a very personable guy. But my mother just loved Michigan Coach Chalmers "Bump" Elliott. My mom also looked into the academics and that sealed the deal. Ohio State is a good school, but it's not Michigan.

Barberton was divided along racial lines, with all of the black families living in an area of the town called "Snydertown." You won't find that name on any map, and there were no Snydertown signs, but people, both black and white, called it that. You knew when you were in Snydertown—the main indication was the roads weren't paved. Race was an issue in Barberton because race was always an issue in the 1960s. A black person didn't walk in a white neighborhood. There

3

was no overriding racial tension in the city. Barberton was primarily a white school system, but in my estimation the black students were treated well.

On the sports fields, there were absolutely no issues. There were only a handful of black players on the team when I played, but Coach Tom "Red" Phillips would not have tolerated any problems. He was a first-rate coach and man. He was an inspirational coach. Throughout the city, there was always racial harmony when it came to athletics, particularly football.

High school football was the No. 1 show on Friday evenings in this community of 35,000, located seven miles from Akron. Every baby boy in Barberton had a football tucked in his bassinet. Every young boy, black and white, dreamed of wearing the purple and white jerseys of the Barberton Magics and playing under the lights at Magic Stadium. It seemed as if everybody in town knew who was playing football and several thousand fans were at the game, and many others were listening on the radio. Barberton had a long athletic tradition. Satchel Page even pitched for a black team located there in the 1930s. But football was Barberton's fall passion.

My football career started in fourth grade at Washington when I was the fullback on a six-man football team wearing only a helmet, shoulder pads and tennis shoes. Money was always tight in our house so I received my equipment one piece at a time. When I finally had the entire run of equipment—including my No. 32 Jim Brown jersey—I slept in full gear. In fact on more than one occasion Momma would have to peel the equipment off me in the middle of the night.

Once I entered U.L. Light Junior High School, I started drawing notice as an athlete. I was a stout lad—not fat, but husky and strong. I scored 32 points in one junior high basketball game, which stood as a school record for exactly 24 hours. The next day, my good buddy Elwood Palmer netted 33 points.

Actually, Bill Taylor didn't officially exist until high school when my football coach started calling me Bill with great regularity.

4

My true name is William Lewis Taylor Jr., and Momma always called me Lewis. In fact, everyone in the family called me Lewis.

My Uncle Eugene had 17 children of his own, but he was a reasonably successful man by our family's standards. He had actually built a duplex house for my mother and her seven kids and Aunt Ernestine and her kids. Aunt Ernestine also had a son named Lewis and he was tagged "Big Lewis" so I became "Little Lewis."

I always knew when I was in trouble with Momma because she would call me "Willie Lewis."

In fourth grade, one of my teachers, Mrs. Shear, called me Bill for the first time.

"I said my name isn't Bill—it's Lewis."

"Your name is William Lewis Taylor," she said. "Bill is short for William."

I didn't like it much. Some kids called me that, but in the neighborhood it was always "Lewis."

My coaches started calling me Bill in the fifth and sixth grade. The name didn't have any staying power until high school when Coach Tom "Red" Phillips started calling me "Bill" on a regular basis.

The young members in my family used to tease me about the name. "Who's Bill," they would say. "Why does he call you that?"

"That's what white folks call someone named William," my Aunt said.

My family was poor financially, but my mother was determined to make sure we were raised with the proper values and morals. In our home, there was a sense of, "we are all in this together." Momma's and Aunt Ernestine's children all worked and contributed to the household income. All of the members of the family went south to pick cotton in the summer. When I was 9 or 10 years old, I worked with family, bringing in the crops on a farm in Hartville, Ohio. The first indication of my athletic prowess came then when I used to run-down rabbits in plowed fields.

"You will never catch that rabbit," my brother would say, as the rabbit would dart between the rows of produce.

"Oh yes I will," I would reply. I had learned quickly that the rabbit would eventually tire before I did. It was difficult for the rabbit to run on the plowed fields.

Momma earned just enough wages at Sam Sing's to keep our heads above water. A large portion of her earnings went to cab fare because Momma didn't drive. But the Sings' were good to our family. I had many meals at the Sing house. Apparently, Momma had learned to drive on my grandfather's Model T Ford, but for some reason had decided it wasn't for her.

Mound Bayou was founded in 1887 by two former slaves: Isaiah T. Montgomery and his cousin Benjamin Green. It was one of the first black towns in America. It became a safe haven for those former slaves seeking relief from the deadly racial violence that marked that part of the country in the post-slavery era. Montgomery, Green, and the other early Black pioneers built the town in the uninhabited wilderness in the Mississippi Delta in Bolivar County. According to the African American Registry, Booker T. Washington participated in some of its economic development, which included the nation's only black-owned cottonseed mill. Mound Bayou also had a train station where the "colored" waiting room was larger than the "white" waiting room, a newspaper, many churches, schools, a bank, a telephone exchange, and other black-owned businesses and industries. Nearly everyone in Mound Bayou could read and write, a remarkable feat, considering that many of the inhabitants at the end of the 19th century were former slaves.

Around 1900, U.S. President Theodore Roosevelt referred to Mound Bayou as "the Jewel of the Delta."

Even today, I can close my eyes and hear my mother talking with poetic fondness about her hometown.

"It's a beautiful city, son," she would say. "You have to go there when you are older. The homes are all beautiful, black people lived very well there. You could walk through the city and you could hear folks chopping steaks in their backyard."

Years later, I did make a trip there and it was just as my mother described it, with its large Victorian houses and rich history overwhelming the city's landscape.

Momma was married three times and gave birth to seven children, four boys and three girls. Her first husband died. She divorced the second one and my father, William Lewis Taylor Sr. died. We were living in Memphis at the time, and my father was working in a sandstone and gravel pit when he suffered a stroke. He was 62 when he died. We moved to Barberton right after that.

Although I have only limited memories of my father, I always felt close to him because Momma told stories about him. It was as if she wanted to make sure that I had a connection to someone that she believed to be a special person. Remember when my father married my mother, he inherited a family with six children.

I am my father's only child. Like the story of Abraham in the Bible, my father had prayed for a son for many years.

My father's prayer to God was that if he had a son, he would "give him back into the hands of the Lord after he is five years old." My mother never understood that part of the prayer until my father died when I was five years old.

What I remember about my father is that he wore railroad clothes and an engineer's cap to match. He was a stocky man with incredible strength—at least he seemed Herculean to me because I could swing from his out-stretched arms. I remember he would always leave me a piece of his sweaty sandwich from his battered lunch pail when he came home from work.

I remember not understanding when I saw his body lying in the casket in the church. "Why is daddy sleeping in the church?" I asked my mother. "He's just resting," she said.

In some respects, I think my mother viewed me as a gift child from God because of my father's prayers. She wanted the best for all of her children—she wanted all of them to find their Mound Bayou—

7

but I always felt as if she expected me to strive for greatness. I was always a good student, as well as a good athlete. I recall, when I was playing football for Michigan, she said to me, "Boy I don't know what to say about you. You may go anywhere and see anything."

That's not to say that I didn't get myself in trouble with Momma from time to time. She wasn't shy about giving me whippings when I deserved them. I might have gotten even more if not for the presence of Aunt Ernestine in our house. I would shake loose from Momma during those whippings and hide under Aunt Ernestine's apron. She called my mother "Kuta" for some reason and she would say. "Kuta, stop whipping that boy." And Momma would cease the whipping.

I recall once hearing Reverend Jesse Jackson giving a speech in which he said that his childhood was spent "in a triangle" formed by church, home and school. That's how my childhood was as well. Aunt Ernestine attended church every Sunday and took us. Momma sometimes didn't go. "Momma is a little tired today," she would say. "I'm going to have church in my heart today."

Momma always did the best she could to keep food on the table. She tried to give us the extras that we all desired, but it wasn't easy. I wanted to learn the piano, so she paid for two lessons because that's all we could afford. Even today, I have a decent ear for music. Back then I played just well enough in junior high school to form a band called "Dramatic Moments." I played the piano. Johnny Walker was the drummer. Elwood Palmer sang. Larry Jones was the lead singer and he had a fine voice. We played at one dance at U.L. Junior High School. We played songs like "Twist and Shout" and "Your Precious Love," plus a couple of Beatles' tunes.

We rarely bought new clothes, but our family always had clean clothes. We had a big black kettle that sat in the backyard. Aunt Ernestine would tell the kids to build a fire under the kettle and all of our clothes were boiled to get them clean. That was our version of a washing machine.

Momma was always very proud of how her children pitched in to contribute. When the house was drafty, my brothers put up paneling to reduce the chill. My oldest brother Felix was already married and moved out when I was relatively young. Jimmy was my oldest brother at home and he was a primary wage earner. He worked as a pinsetter at Ralph's Bowling Alley. Many of the black youngsters worked as pinsetters. Whether it was raining or cold as ice, Jimmy walked to work. He always said he was the "best pin setter in the world." Before days of automation, a pinsetter would jump into the pit between every roll and clean out the fallen pins and prepare for the next ball. To be honest it was dangerous work because sometimes-mischievous white teen-agers would purposely throw a shot down the alley when Jimmy was in there just to see him have to dive out of the way.

Once, when I was there watching that happened and I was so mad because these white boys were laughing about it. I wanted to go after them, and Jimmy held me back. "Let it alone," he said. "You are just going to create more trouble."

Momma admired Jimmy greatly because he always brought home every cent he earned. He never asked for any of the money.

Jimmy was the slimmest youngster I ever saw in my entire life. If he turned sideways, you could lose sight of him. Growing up, I always knew I was going to get a meal and three-quarters of a meal because Jimmy hardly ever ate. He would have a few bites, light up a cigarette and he would be off to see some girl.

The other physical characteristic he had was his gigantic hands. The joints of his fingers were swollen the size of Ping Pong balls. He used those giant hands to "squench" my head—which was squeezing it between his two palms. I always looked to Momma to rescue me, but she would always be laughing. "Now Jimmy is a working man," she would say. "I'm just going to leave him alone."

Jimmy's last name was Jackson. My other brother at home was Thomas Jackson, who died a few years ago of leukemia. His nicknames were "Black Jack, Catfish or Jackson."

Thomas was the "Dennis the Menace" of our family. He was always getting himself into one pickle or another. He was often guilty of unauthorized borrowing of his brothers' clothes and personal effects, which often turned our house into a battleground.

Once I put a red and white sweater into layaway at the J.C. Penny store and paid on it regularly through the wages I earned. I was so proud of that sweater when I finally finished paying for it.

I was going to wear it for the first time on a movie date with a junior high school cheerleader. But when I got home the sweater was missing from my dresser. I waited for Thomas on the porch with a baseball bat. That night Momma intervened before the fight ever really got started. In fact, I got in the most trouble for calling him a "sucker."

Nevertheless, it wasn't settled and the next day we tangled over the sweater. I didn't even want that sweater after he had worn it. During the fight, he had pinned me and then let me up and started running. I picked up a brick and hit him in the back of the head. Then I did an about-face and was on the run with a bloody Thomas chasing after me. I ran into the house and into the kitchen where I slid under Momma's apron like a runner sliding into second base.

Momma jumped in surprise and nearly knocked a pot off the stove. I was crying, but inside I was feeling quite satisfied about connecting with my well-aimed throw.

Although he was bleeding, Thomas was not hurt as much as he was angry and revengeful.

"You had no business messing with my stuff," I yelled. "That's what you get."

"I'm going to get you when you come outside," he screamed back.

Momma looked at both of us and said, "Ain't nobody going to get nobody."

Jackson then said, "Yes I am."

That was a mistake. Momma did not allow her children to sass her. She unloaded on him with a slap to the side of the head. Joe Louis couldn't have landed a blow any harder.

Even I felt sorry for Thomas. She told him to stop picking on me, and she told me that if I didn't stop throwing things I was going to get my head rammed into a wall. Momma was a dear, sweet lady, but she was a tough disciplinarian. In those days, parents in our neighborhood all believed that you couldn't spare the rod. Parents of my friends thought nothing of whipping me if I got out of line. They knew that Momma would thank them for doing it. And when I got home, I would get whipped again for misbehaving at my friend's home.

My brothers and I were all about five years apart in age, but within a couple of years I was much bigger than Thomas. He learned to respect me then.

By the time I arrived in high school, coaches were excited about my football potential. I played varsity as a sophomore, but not much as a running back. We had John Varge in the backfield, and he was a good back. He's a principal now at Barberton High School. I played defensive back and ran back some kicks. But coaches clearly were penciling me in as a starting running back as a junior before Momma decided I couldn't play.

Truthfully, Momma didn't give me permission to play football as a senior, as much as she just didn't strongly forbid me to play. "I saw how sad you were," she said.

I had learned to cut hair, and was earning decent money, 50 cents or one dollar a cut. At that time, I was considering becoming a barber. However, Coach Phillips told me before my senior season, "You have a chance to play college football. You aren't going to cut hair."

As I recall, Barberton was 6-2-1 in my senior season. Recruiters started to notice me as the season wore on. Pat Coughenour was the quarterback on that team. He went on to play defensive back in college for Akron.

To be honest, my memories of that season are blurry, but teammates Danny Otto supplied some newspaper clippings from that time that indicate that I rushed for about 1,000 yards. Another buddy, Ron Grinder, who played on that team, also has helped me fill in the gaps of my memory of my high school career.

In one article, Phillips is quoted as saying I was "the best runner" he ever had. At that time, I rushed for 800 yards in 144 attempts, plus 12 touchdowns. I had 145 yards against Cuyahoga Falls. Against Buchtel High School, I ran for 249 yards in 34 carries and 2 touchdowns. That was the second-to-last game of the season and recruiters took note of that performance.

"I shudder to think what the season would be without (Taylor)," Phillips said in the article.

One memory I do have of that season is Momma's one trip to Magic Stadium to see me play.

Her great fear was that I was going to get hurt, and of course, the one game she attended during my senior year was the one game where I was injured.

After taking a big hit, I recall being in tremendous pain while sprawled on the turf, but I remember thinking, *If I don't get up Momma is never going to let me play football again!*

It didn't help that the stadium announcer informed the crowd, "That's Bill Taylor who is hurt on the play."

What I didn't know was that my brothers were trying to distract Momma, pointing out different people in the stands and making small talk. But at one point Momma said, "Did someone just say that Bill Taylor was hurt?"

I honestly don't remember what injury I had, but I do recall that I decided I was getting up and walking off that field. If I had broken my leg, I think I would have gotten up and walked to prevent Momma from worrying.

Although Momma wouldn't allow us to watch football on our black and white television, I would sneak off to watch it at my friends' homes. I was a rabid Browns fan. I can still name the team's starting lineups from the 1960s. I loved Jimmy Brown, Gene Hickerson, Ray Renfro and Milt Plum. In my mind, Jim Brown is the greatest running back in NFL history.

What I loved about Brown is that when he got up from a heavy hit, he looked like he could barely walk. Nevertheless, on the next play, he would plow through the line like he was a Sherman Tank.

Barberton had a history for producing football talent. Former NFL coach John Mackovic played at Barberton. In fact, his half-brother Larry North played with me. He was a good player. Quarterback George Izzo played at Barberton High School from 1954-1956. At the NFL level, George Izzo tied a league record by throwing a 99-yard touchdown pass for the Washington Redskins against my Cleveland Browns in 1963.

Although I had 57 college scholarship offers, I whittled down my choices to Ohio State, Michigan, Cornell and West Virginia. I know I might have gone to Cornell had that school had football scholarships. The school was going to give me an academic scholarship, but it didn't seem as guaranteed as a full-ride football scholarship. I was also very impressed with West Virginia's program, particularly coach Jim Karlin. He's the one that bolstered my confidence about playing college football.

"I'm not going to beat around the bush with you," Karlin said. "I've watched a lot of your films and you can play with anyone in the country."

To be honest, I was born with an inward cockiness for athletics, but everyone has self-doubt. You just wonder if there are other players out there that are much better than you are. When Coach Karlin said what he did, I was ready to play college football.

As I reflect on that time in my life, I realize there were a multitude of factors pointing me toward Ann Arbor. The incident with Woody was important, certainly. And Momma did like Bump Elliot when she talked to him on the phone. But Coach Phillips had told me to go where I felt comfortable.

"Remember this is going to be where you spend the next four years of your life," Coach Phillips had said. "If you aren't happy, it's going to be a bad experience."

Michigan did seem like a good fit for me. I just liked the Ann Arbor campus, the atmosphere and the people. Moreover, Bump was running the "I formation" and that was appealing. Also in 1967, Michigan assistant coach Tony Mason had brought Wolverines' basketball star Cazzie Russell to Barberton in connection with the founding of a chapter of the Fellowship of Christian Athletes. I joined during my senior year and I still remember Mason's speech. He was a gifted orator, free flowing with his analogies and ideas. He forced you to consider your opinions, goals and dreams.

"Anyone can be average," he said. "If you can breathe you are average. You must strive to be above average at whatever pursuit you have in mind."

He brought home the point with style and strength. "If you are going to have open heart surgery, do you want an average doctor performing the operation?" he asked. "Do you want a guy that thinks to himself, it doesn't matter whether I win or I lose the patient, it's how I make that cut that counts. No you don't. You want a winner in that operating room. You want someone who is going to push himself to be the best surgeon he can be."

As I recall Tony Mason ended up being a head coach at Cincinnati and Arizona. His speech had a profound impact on me.

I did have one memorable recruiting trip, during my senior year while in Miami. Thom Darden, a top player from Sandusky, Ohio, and I both ended up visiting Miami on the same weekend. As a Barberton player, I owed it to my school to look at Miami. The coach there was Bo Schembechler who was from Barberton. His mom still worked at the First National Bank in Barberton where my mother had a savings account. Often my mother would ask her about one of Barberton's most famous sons. When I was nine or ten years old, I actually met Coach Schembechler when I was in the First National Bank with my mother.

To me, the trip made sense, because Bo was a Barberton native and everyone told me I should at least check out his program. Darden and I already knew each other from previous recruiting trips. We figured we would have some fun together because recruiting trips were primarily designed to impress upon athletes how much fun could be had while playing football at the school. You usually met some coeds, and attended a couple of parties with football players.

But Schembechler's recruiting visit wasn't like any of the other trips we had taken.

We arrived in Oxford, Ohio, on a Friday afternoon. It started the way they all started. We met the coaches, had dinner, drove around the campus and talked football and academics. We later met some of Bo's players, went to a movie and met some coeds and stayed up late.

However, the whole tone changed the next morning when Bo and his assistant coaches rousted us out of bed at 6:00 in the morning. They said we were going to work out. We all looked at each other and I was thinking, *you got to be kidding me!* No schools ever worked out the recruits. But Bo Schembechler did. We showered, dressed in shorts, T-shirts and sneakers, wolfed down cereal and were escorted to the gym for weight-lifting, sprints for time, distance running and a game of basketball against some of his varsity players. "I want to see what kind of quickness you have," Bo said.

At one point, Bo walked over and squeezed my biceps. "You're soft, out of shape Taylor," he said. "When we get you here, we will get you in shape."

When our times didn't live up to his expectation he chastised us. "How did you guys score all of those touchdowns and make all those big plays when you're dead tired from a light warm-up?" he snorted.

Honestly, we couldn't wait to exit that gym and as soon as were out of his earshot we cursed in all of the creative ways we had at our disposal.

"That man is crazy," I told Darden. He didn't dispute that assessment. Both of us agreed we weren't coming to Oxford to play "for this maniac."

When Schembechler called the house, I didn't return his calls. When he sent letters, I didn't open them. His assistant coaches also didn't get their calls returned. I wanted to make it clear that I had no interest in going to Miami. Anybody who asked me about Miami, I told them straight out, "Don't go there 'cuz the program is run by a crazy man."

After Thom and I signed our letters of intent with Michigan, we didn't give any further thought to Schembechler or his program at Miami. We didn't pay attention when his Miami squad posted a 7-3 record in 1968, while surrendering just 99 points in 10 games. We didn't know that several high profile programs had Schembechler at the top of the list of coaching candidates.

During my freshman year at Michigan, we learned that Elliott was stepping down as coach to become Don Canham's assistant in the athletic office. However, I wasn't prepared for the headlines in the *Akron Beacon Journal* one morning when I was back in Barberton over Christmas vacation.

"Schembechler named head football coach at Michigan," the headline screamed.

If I had been eating Corn Flakes at the time, I would have spit them out. It was almost too goofy to be believed. It was like a plot from a situation-comedy, when the man you despise the most ends up becoming your boss. To anyone else it would seem humorous, but I kept thinking that my career might be over before it started at Michigan. If Schembechler was mad at me for snubbing him, he certainly wasn't going to push me to the top of his depth chart. With Ron Johnson graduating, it was going to be a wide-open competition for the No. 1 tailback job in my sophomore season. Would he give me a chance when I wouldn't even return his phone calls the spring before?

What I didn't know was that Bo had a sense of humor about the situation. When we returned to Ann Arbor for the second semester, he scheduled a one-on-one meeting with each of his players.

When I walked into his office, his grin was as wide as the doorway. "Hot damn Taylor, you thought we were going to get away from me, didn't you?" he said, laughter filling the room. Apparently, he had the same conversation with Darden.

Then Bo's tone turned serious. "Taylor, we are both from Barberton and we both have to prove ourselves here," he said. "Hell, these people can't even pronounce my name. They think I'm some kind of Mid-American fool trying to step up into the mighty Big Ten."

He looked me at me as if he was a general sending me on a combat mission. "Taylor, you can't just be a good back at Michigan," he said. "You have to be a great back. I'm going to push you harder than you have ever been pushed before."

When the conversation was over, I didn't know whether to be elated or scared out of my mind. Obviously, I was still in his plans. But I also knew that he had a reputation as one of the toughest taskmasters in the game. The word was that his practices were grueling and his demeanor was frighteningly harsh. I had gotten a taste of that at Miami and now I was going to swallow his entire program. I knew I faced a mountainous challenge. What I didn't know was that Bo would be my mentor and friend for going on 40 years.

CHAPTER 2

BILLY TAYLOR / GENERAL BO

W̲HEN M̲ICHIGAN C̲OACH B̲O S̲CHEMBECHLER was at his best, he was one part comedian, two parts Vince Lombardi, three parts General George Patton with just a dash of Winston Churchill and a hint of a crazy man.

One of my favorite memories is Bo standing in front of us while pretending to be praying to the Sun God. As we all took a knee, sweating and gasping for air in the stifling August heat in Ann Arbor, Bo would be raising his hands to the heavens.

"Oh Sun we pray that you will beat down upon us," he would say as if he was reciting a prayer. "We need 100 degrees to get us in shape. We need you to turn up the heat because we have to be ready for the Big Ten season. We want 100 degrees because we know it's good for us. It will make us strong."

He would stop in the middle of beseeching the Sun God to ask a player or two if he also was praying for hotter weather.

"Dierdorf you want it hotter don't you?" Bo would say.

"Yes, sir I want it hotter," Dierdorf would say.

No one was going to undermine Schembechler's motivational skit. But privately, a few of the guys would be whispering, "This man is crazy."

Shortly after Schembechler was hired, he came in and ran winter conditioning.

It was like a military boot camp. None of us had ever participated in training like this. Vomiting was simply part of the program because Bo ran us so hard. It seemed as if we were preparing for a marathon instead of a football season. If I'm not mistaken, I recall that he wanted his backs to run a mile under five minutes and 30 seconds. If someone was struggling to complete the runs, his teammates weren't allowed to assist him. "Leave him alone," Bo would yell. Then he would go over and tell the fallen player, in the unkindest way possible, to get back up and keep running. I'm not exaggerating when I say that about one-third of the players quit, including some juniors and seniors. As a freshman, I didn't know enough to complain. I didn't know that Bo was being tougher on his players than former coach Bump Elliott had been. I just did what the coach asked in conditioning and spring practice.

"No prima donnas on this team," Bo would scream.

We all had to look up what a "prima donna" was, because we weren't sure. Frequently he would call us "ham and eggers" because he said we're too accustomed to the soft life.

When Bo's players look back on his first pre-season conditioning program, we talk as if we were survivors of some battle or military engagement.

"It was basically a war," Thom Darden always says.

Bo really loved one drill that we called the "Stomp and Slap." Players were ordered to climb into a boxing ring for a one-on-one confrontation with another player. The idea was to stomp on your opponent's foot and then smack him. The objective was to develop better hand-eye-coordination, and improved quickness of the feet and toughness. Bo really especially liked to see the linemen in this drill because it simulated one-on-one encounters in the trenches.

None of the survivors will forget the time that defensive end Cecil Pryor was competing in this drill against a walk-on and the competition escalated into combat. The walk-on put a good smack on

Pryor, and Cecil threw his gloves down and started pummeling the kid.

Bo jumped into the ring, grabbed Pryor, and yelled. "C'mon Pryor if you want to fight someone, you can fight me."

All of us were flabbergasted that our coach was willing to break-up that fight and challenge Cecil who was quite a physical presence.

Bo would also say that "those who stay will be champions." His prediction was accurate, although it was difficult for us to envision our rosy future, given our state of exhaustion. However, looking back, I think we all respected Bo for what he was trying to do. At the time, there was a general feeling that Michigan needed to improve its toughness if it wanted to win championships.

Maybe some of the freshmen were more prepared for the winter conditioning than upperclassmen because freshmen only play a two-game schedule. The rest of the fall, we just practiced and beat up on each other. We were coached by Bill Dodd who closely resembled Robert Conrad from the *Wild Wild West TV* show. Dodd was a former Marine, and he ran practice like a drill instructor.

Every week the freshmen played in what we called the "Toilet Bowl." It was a controlled scrimmage against the Michigan first-team offense and defense. It felt as if we were just fresh meat for the Wolverines. They tore us up every week, although I did manage to break a couple of long runs against the first team defense. Nobody was thrilled about playing in that scrimmage against the varsity, but we knew it was important to look as sharp as we could to impress the varsity coaches. As freshmen, we smacked around each other every day in preparation for a game, but there were only two games against Bowling Green and Toledo. (My first collegiate touchdown came against Bowling Green). We disliked Coach Dodd mostly because we thought it was silly to be hitting all the time when there were no games. We were getting hurt for no reason but in hindsight, he may have prepared us for Schembechler's winter training regimen.

The good news for me heading into the 1969 season was that Ron Johnson had graduated, meaning there was an opening to be the No. 1

tailback. In spring practice, I believed I had made a strong case to be his heir apparent. However, in the first week of fall training camp, I suffered a separated shoulder when Wolfman Frank Gusich made a great hit and he drove my shoulder into the turf.

What I remember is that a trainer had to place his foot on my chest to get the leverage needed to pull that shoulder back in place. I ended up with my shoulder wrapped in a figure eight style bandage, and placed in a harness. I simply didn't have the opportunity to compete with my buddy Glenn Doughty for the No. 1 tailback job.

Going into the season, *The Detroit Free Press* billed Doughty "as the new Ron Johnson."

If you think that made me angry, you are mistaken. When I was recruited at Michigan, I was one of seven African American players brought in on scholarship. We represented the largest black recruiting class the school had ever known. The group included Doughty from Detroit, defensive back Thom Darden from Sandusky, Ohio, guard Reggie McKenzie from Highland Park, Michigan, wide receiver Mike Oldham from Cincinnati, linebacker Mike Taylor from Detroit, defensive end Butch Carpenter from Flint and me.

Bump Elliott had done me a real service by rooming me with Ron Johnson, plus other black players Marty Washington, George Hoey and Warren Sipp during my freshman year. I think he wanted me to see that other black athletes were fitting in well and having fun on campus. But I had an instant rapport with the other black players in my class. It didn't take long until we were branding ourselves, "The Mellow Men." We were kind of like a fraternity without the charter or desire to expand our membership. We were a tight group. Even our parents became friends. We had overflowing pride in our association and we looked after each other. We cheered for each other sincerely.

"You guys are special and if you stick together you will make history," Butch Carpenter's father told us.

Doughty was probably the team's best all-around athlete. I think Bo even said that publicly. I believed I was a better runner than Doughty was, but he was a more efficient blocker and he could catch the football. He was a little faster in a sprint than I was. Actually what Bo really liked about Doughty was his attitude. He was gung-ho on every play. He was always puffed up and loud.

In those first two games of the 1969 season, Doughty rushed for a total of 329 yards and did look like he could be another Johnson. In fact, his 80-yard touchdown run against Vanderbilt in the season opener was eight yards longer than Johnson's longest TD jaunt. Doughty's dash was the fourth longest run in Michigan history, behind Tom Harmon's 86-yard run in 1940, Bill Culligan's 85-yard run in 1944 and Mel Anthony's 84-yard rumble in 1965. When Doughty scored, I was among the first guys to congratulate him. He was one of the best friends I had on the team.

In Johnson's first two games on varsity, he gained 355 yards on 45 carries. Doughty had his 329 on 44 carries. But Johnson was a junior on his first Michigan carries, while Glenn was a sophomore.

Glenn tried to divert attention from his accomplishments, telling reporters, "I know I can't replace Johnson. I'm just trying to do the best I can."

Bo told reporters that two games "doesn't make a season," but he admitted that Doughty had developed quickly. Purdue coach Jack Mollenkopf said Doughty reminded him of the notable Boilermakers' running back Leroy Keyes.

"He runs with authority," Bo said. "The first guy who has a chance of getting him doesn't usually get him. That's a mark of a good runner."

As a sophomore, I was reading everything Bo had to say because I wanted to figure out exactly how he wanted me to play. Although Glenn had a great start, I just figured I would get my opportunity at some point. I knew I had to be prepared.

After missing two games because of my shoulder injury, I willed myself ready for action in game 3 against Missouri. I probably came back too early, but I wanted a chance to prove myself to Bo.

"Remember, Taylor," he reminded me as I prepared to play, "You can't just be a good back. You have to be a great back."

Unfortunately, my debut performance didn't match my enthusiasm. The record shows that I fumbled on my first collegiate carry against the Tigers on October 4, 1969. I was carrying the ball off tackle when a linebacker smacked me squarely on my injured left shoulder. The ball popped out as I was going down. I was in a fair amount of pain, but all I could think about was, *Bo is going to have a fit. The man is going to kill me*! When you play for Bo Schembechler, you don't fumble. He expects you to protect the ball as if it is your child. When I was lying on that ground, I wanted to dig a hole to the center of the earth. According to the official statistics, I ended up with two carries for one yard in that game. I didn't get much playing time after that fumble. Bo was in a foul mood after that game because we lost 31-20 at home. It was his first loss as Michigan's coach. He said he had never had one of his teams perform as poorly as we had performed. I was reasonably sure that my fumble was at the top of his list of major mistakes. Now in addition to everything else, I had to concern myself with as a sophomore, I had to prove I could hang onto to the ball.

Bo made it clear that I had much to prove. Before the next game against Purdue, he came over after I had my shoulder taped and said, "Are sure you can handle it, Taylor."

That was all part of Bo's psychology. He wanted you to know that he was doubting you because he believed it would inspire you to a peak performance. In my case, it worked. On my first play in that game, Bo called the "57 tailback draw" and I broke one for over 20 yards. My final tally was 53 yards in 13 carries. More importantly, I didn't fumble the football. I held onto the ball so tightly that it was more or less attached to my body.

Although I ran the ball hard against Purdue, the feeling among the coaches was that I was rushing myself back. It was decided I would not play against Michigan State.

We lost 23-12 at East Lansing, and there was injury added to the insult. Doughty came up lame after the game, and doctors said he couldn't play the next game on the road against Minnesota. Bo found a novel way of telling me I had been promoted to No. 1 tailback.

"Michigan State has Eric Allen, Ohio State has Jim Otis and John Brockington, and I'm stuck with Taylor as my starting running back," said Bo as we started practice that week. "I might have the worst backfield in the Big Ten this week."

But he looked me sternly in the eye and said, "But Bill, we are going to show them something in Minnesota, aren't we?"

The Michigan record was only 3-2 at that point in the season, and Bo might have been looking for a way to re-energize our team. Even then, I had this feeling that Bo believed in my ability to create big plays. I wasn't afraid heading into my first start, but I was extremely nervous to the point that I couldn't eat my pre-game meal. Middle guard Henry Hill was the first one to notice I had some butterflies.

"If you aren't going to eat that damn steak, pass it over here," Hill said to me. "What's the matter with you?"

He stabbed the meat with his fork and began to chow down. As he did, he began to counsel me.

"Are you worried about this damn game?" Hill asked.

My silence answered his question.

"Look, I can understand you being nervous because I started as a sophomore too," he said. "And people used to tease me because I was short, and your little short ass is shorter than I am."

Now he was laughing. "But you just go out there and show them that the little man can play the game. Shit, just run the damn ball like you do in practice. You come at us hard. To tell you the truth, I don't even like to tackle your short, stocky ass."

That's the way Henry Hill talked, direct and colorful. He wasn't through lecturing. "I've played a few games now and I haven't come up against people that run any tougher than you do," he said. "And if you can run up against our defense in practice, you can run against any team in the country."

Right before the start of the game, Hill approached and pointed his finger into my helmet. "Don't forget what I told you," he said. "We are going to kick their ass."

That was Hill's way of patting me on the back. That was his way of saying, "Let it all hang out, Billy."

In the opening series, I popped a couple of dudes, and broke some tackles. I was feeling confident. I caught a pass in the flat and turned it into a 10-yard touchdown reception. When the game was over, I had rushed for 151 yards and two other touchdowns. I found some daylight in those games, but it wasn't one of my longer runs that I remember most about that game.

Early in the second quarter of that game, quarterback Don Moorhead handed me the ball and two Minnesota linebackers were in the backfield quick enough to knock me half way to North Dakota. A few screws came loose as I hit the ground. When I was able to refocus, I saw Bo standing over me, screaming, "Great play Taylor. Great Play Taylor. Now that's playing football. Great play."

Honestly, I believed the man had lost his mind. He hated negative yardage, and pushed us to fire into that hole with reckless abandon. Bad blocking or good blocking, Bo expected his backs to be able to gain yardage.

When I came to the sideline, he put his arm around me and said, "Taylor, you don't even know why that was a great play, do you?

"To tell you the truth coach no I don't," I admitted.

"You held onto to the football," Schembechler said. "You didn't fumble. I don't know if anyone else could have held on to that football after that kind of hit."

He walked away, and I continued to believe he was nuts. Remember this was my first game as a starter and I really didn't know yet what Bo was all about. All I knew is that I was running, blocking, catching a touchdown pass against Minnesota, and he thought my best effort came on a play in which I lost a couple of yards.

That game was the turning point of my entire Michigan career. There were questions about my ability going into that game. Those doubts were erased when the game was over. I know whatever butterflies I had before the game were gone by the first quarter. I found confidence against Minnesota, and I carried that confidence forward. Over a four-game span, I rushed for 673 yards.

Because that game against Minnesota was on the road, there was a buzz about me going into our homecoming game against Wisconsin. I have a tape from WAAM radio on which the announcers say, "The Michigan faithful can't wait to see who this Billy Taylor really is."

I showed fans I wasn't the same tentative runner they saw perform against Missouri. Against the Badgers, I bulled my way for 152 yards on just 15 carries. The following week I had an 84-yard touchdown gallop at Illinois, which is still one of the longest runs in Michigan history. At the time, it tied Anthony's run for the third longest at Michigan.

What I remember most about that run was that it came on a warm day in Illinois and I was losing steam as I raced toward the end zone. I slowed down, running just fast enough to prevent anyone from catching me. I was tuckered out when I crossed the goal line. I remember Dan Dierdorf almost crushing me when he hugged me in celebration. My teammates mobbed me, and I was trying to push everyone away because it was difficult to breathe.

During that run, it felt as if I were carrying a baby grand piano on my back, but Schembechler was thinking much larger. "Damn Taylor, get in shape," Bo screamed. "You looked like you were going to die before you reached the end zone. You looked like you were carrying a truck on your back."

Certainly, I wasn't the only player singled out for Bo's criticism. Bo's doghouse was always standing room only. He was always riding Thom Darden about missed tackles, and any member of our team at that time should be able to recite the speech that Schembechler always gave Thom during a game: "Darden get the ball. We need the ball. Make a play. Do something out there!"

Occasionally, Bo would surprise you with a compliment. When you received one, it felt like you had been knighted. My highest single game production was 225 yards against Iowa in my sophomore season. At one point early in the game, we were in a fourth-and-nine situation at about the Iowa 30 and Bo called for a tailback draw. Getting into my stance, I remember feeling honored that Bo had enough confidence to call my number in a passing down. I also felt some trepidation that he would blame me if the play failed. As it turned out, the play did succeed. I spun off tackle, and probably broke five tackles en route to the end zone. I sidestepped a defensive back just before I crossed the goal line.

When the team was watching the film, Bo became very excited during that run. "Damn, Taylor," he said, "Where did you learn to run like that?"

As our season wore on, the Mellow Men became even closer and our friendship became a focal point of the team. Everyone knew who the Mellow Men were, and by the end of our sophomore season, we decided we wanted to live together. We found a six-bedroom house on Geddes, near the corner of the Observatory. We formulated a plan to convince the Michigan athletic department to give us permission to rent it.

This was the time of the Black Action Movement, and Bo was always concerned that we might become too politically involved and lose our focus on football. But more importantly, Bo would have been more worried that we would get ourselves into trouble with too much partying. We actually decided to tell a little "white lie" to Athletic Director Don Canham to achieve our objective. Actually, in hindsight, it was a whopper of a lie.

We chose Mike Oldham and Butch Carpenter to talk to Canham because they were the two guys in our group who most closely resembled model citizens. If Darden or I would have gone to make our case, Canham might have been suspicious of our intent. If Canham looked at me, he would be thinking it was going to be a party house. When he looked at Carpenter and Oldham, he saw two clean-cut kids with an organized plan. Butch was probably the most practical and responsible man in the group, and Oldham looked conservative in his manner and dress.

Darden always told the story of meeting Oldham for the first time in a recruiting visit to Ann Arbor. He remembers seeing this well-dressed young man with his group, "looking older and more dignified than the rest of us."

Finally, Darden said to Oldham, "Are you a coach?"

Oldham started laughing. "Nah man I'm a player just like you."

Canham had to sign off on the move because of our scholarship situation and we had anticipated his line of questioning. We were prepared for the ultimate question.

"Is Bo okay with this?" Canham asked.

"He said it's fine," Carpenter and Oldham lied.

There was the whopper lie. We didn't talk to Bo about it because we were fearful he would say 'no'. If our lie was discovered, nothing was ever said to us about it. And in our junior season, the Den of the Mellow Men almost became an institution on campus. Reporters wrote about it, and players talked about it.

Some of the white players on the team would hang out with us in the Den. Linebacker/kicker Dana Coin would always be at the party with the brothers and sisters. "I'm going to be a Mellow Man," he would say.

By the time we were juniors, the Mellow Men were in a leadership position and the 1971 team would end up being "our team."

Essentially, the Mellow Men grew up in that house. Thom Darden was an only-child and he often talks about how living with the Mellow Men helped him learn to share and to be more self-sufficient.

Egos never got in the way. If they ever did, McKenzie would have gotten us back in line. We always said that McKenzie was our sergeant at arms because he was the biggest and strongest among us. He was a tough man. When he would be rumbling up field zeroing in on a defender, I'm sure more than one linebacker or defensive back made his peace with God before the collision. McKenzie's blocks were like car crashes. Running backs would all joke about "getting up in McKenzie's ass pocket" and riding his block for good yardage. Running behind McKenzie was like catching a good wave in surfing. It could be a helluva ride. Mike Taylor, no relation to me, was also a rough and tumble guy. Darden, who would eventually become an All-Pro in the NFL, says Taylor was the "smartest defensive player on our team." He wasn't a big linebacker by today's standards, but he knew how to keep linemen off of him.

It took a while for Oldham to loosen up. He wore his white shirts and wing-tip shoes for a while, but over time we got him to enjoy a beer and grow some sideburns. We used to jokingly say he was "L7." If you don't get that reference, look at what an L and 7 fused together forms—it's a square.

I don't think we ever convinced Butch Carpenter to drink, not even for a toast. But he may have been the most popular guy in the group. He liked the parties, but he didn't like the drinking. He's 6-foot 2-inches and I probably weighed as much as he did. He was a skinny defensive end, but he always got the job done.

We could kid each other like that because we respected and admired each other. I would have done anything for any of the Mellow Men back in our glory days. We would sit around as a group and discuss problems, or what was happening on campus. The Michigan campus was a lightning rod for what was happening around the world. We felt fortunate to be on the campus at the time we were there. It was such an incredible mix of radical ideas and educational values. Darden could walk through a war protest on the way to his Econ 101 class, where he would be taught by a professor who was on the economic committee for President Richard Nixon. Every time you walked around campus, you should have been earning college credits, because you learned so much about world issues. When you strolled through The Diag, you would hear about Gay rights, nuclear proliferation and Vietnam. We saw women burning their bras. We saw streakers. It was a wild scene for a kid from Barberton. It's a good thing Momma didn't walk through the Diag. She might have made me come home.

The Den of the Mellow Men was famous for our parties, and for the number of women that paraded in and out of our place. However, we had rules, and we lived by those rules. Every Friday during the football season, we came home after practice to clean the Den. The house was a wreck for six days, but we wanted it nice for Saturday because that's when our parents would visit after the game. They would bring plenty of soul food and we would all have a great time.

However, I have to be truthful and say that we always looked forward to the time that the parents kissed us goodbye because then we could bring the girls in.

We had an exceptional team in 1969, but everyone in college football believed Ohio State had a better squad. In 1968, the Buckeyes had won the national championship with Rex Kern at quarterback. The team was 8-0, ranked No. 1 and coming into Ann Arbor for the last game in 1969. Buckeyes' coach Woody Hayes had said earlier in the season that he believed his 1969 team was a better team than the 1968 team. The Buckeyes had a 22-game winning streak coming into this game, including 17 consecutive Big Ten wins.

We truly expected to beat the Buckeyes. Family would call me from Barberton and ask whether I thought Michigan had a chance against the Buckeyes.

"Have a chance, nothing—we will be beat them," I would say.

That was Bo talking through me. He began convincing us we would conquer Ohio State at the beginning of the season. And right after I moved to tailback, we had really started to click as a football team. We were 4-0 and our offense had really begun to click.

Bo insisted all season that our big game would be the last game against Ohio State, and we were going to beat the Buckeyes. We played one game at a time that season, but always in the back of our minds, we prepared for Woody Hayes and Ohio State. Guys from the Den of the Mellow Men were all starters as sophomores, and we were playing with a great group of seniors like Dan Dierdorf, Garvie Craw,

Jim Mandich, Don Moorhead and Cecil Pryor. Moorhead was a tough competitor at quarterback. Bo nicknamed him "Warbler" because he mumbled in the huddle and we all had a difficult time understanding him in the beginning of the season. Mandich would go on to have a great career in the NFL with the Miami Dolphins. He was an exceptional receiver, and a relentless blocker.

None of the newspapers, even in Detroit and Ann Arbor, believed we had any chance to beat Ohio State. In one newspaper I read, "Michigan had two chances of winning this game, slim and none."

We were all ready for Bo to talk to us, like he always did before a game, especially a big game like this. We expected a long oration. However, it didn't happen.

First he said, "These guys from Columbus are coming into our house and they are strutting about like they own the place."

Second, he pointed out that they were wearing white shoes and that irritated him.

Finally, he turned the bill of cap his to the back and said, "Our own newspapers are saying our chances of winning this game are slim and none." He glared around the room slowly. "I'll tell you what, we are going to go out there and kick their ass." He slammed the chalkboard with his fist and knocked it over. Everyone had tears in their eyes.

There is a fine line between lunacy and being fired up to play football. We were straddling that line. I remember guys like Pryor and Craw were throwing around chairs.

You had to be a real man to force your way out of the Michigan locker room that day. Players were pushing to get out of the door. When we took the field, no one felt like his feet touched the ground. Everyone flying out of that dressing room seemed to have gained super powers. To this day, I've never seen a Michigan team that came together like we did in that game. Sometimes in a game, the offense doesn't show up until the second quarter or the defense doesn't show up at all. It's difficult to have everyone playing well at the same time. However, in this game, we all were there from the beginning.

In those days, I think there was a metal floor in the stadium and the noise level was incredible. You couldn't hear yourself talk when you got onto the field. Even when Ohio State scored first, we knew we were going to win. It was 24-12 at halftime, and that's how it stayed. I have a videotape of that game, and up and down the line on offense and defense, Michigan players were at the top of their game. What a great team game we played.

When the game was over, Craw told then *Detroit Free Press* sports editor Joe Falls that the triumph was "the greatest victory in the history of the world."

Perhaps that was an exaggeration, but in our post-game celebration, it felt as if we had just won a war. I've known Bo for 37 years, and I don't know if I've ever seen him more joyous than he was after we defeated No. 1 Ohio State. When we sang the Victors' song, he was in a booming voice. He may have sung it louder and prouder than any player.

Remember, Bo is a native Ohioan and he had coached under Woody Hayes at Ohio State. This game was very personal to Bo and me. I gained 84 yards in this game, including a 28-yard run to set-up a short touchdown plunge by Craw that helped us come from behind. We trailed twice in that game, and each time we came back. Barry Pierson had three interceptions and returned a punt 60 yards to help our cause. Moorhead out-performed Kern at quarterback.

"I think Bo has Woody's number," Craw told Falls. "The Buckeyes didn't do a thing that our coach didn't tell us they would do. Bo is going to be coach of the year. If he doesn't win a million awards, it will be a sin."

If we could have duplicated the effort we put forth against Ohio State, we would have beaten Southern California in the Rose Bowl.

But what happened in Pasadena the day before the Rose Bowl made that game seem meaningless. As soon as we came together for a meeting the morning of the game and there was no Bo, we all knew something was wrong. You could hear the murmuring that was rippling through the players as Assistant Coach Jerry Hanlon made some points about the game as if this was a normal meeting. But I think he had tears in his eyes, as I recall. And the other coaches were like zombies. Their bodies were there, but they looked pale and somber. There was no determination in their voices about the upcoming football game.

Finally, we were informed that Bo had suffered a heart attack. Defensive coordinator Jim Young assumed the coaching responsibilities, but it really didn't matter. Vince Lombardi, Tom Landry and the ghost of Knute Rockne could have coached our team, and it would not have made a difference. We were defeated as soon as we received the news about Bo.

The players' minds were not on that game. We lost 10-3 on a third quarter 33-yard touchdown pass from Jimmy Jones to Bob Chandler. I suffered a pinched nerve in that game, and finished with 56 yards on 18 carries. In the week leading up to the Rose Bowl, Glenn Doughty suffered a knee injury that was severe enough that surgery was required in the off-season. But the injuries weren't nearly as critical as the mental devastation that we suffered.

No one is invincible. But Bo was irreplaceable. If the Wolverines lost Moorhead, we still had a chance of winning. If we lost me at tailback, we still had a chance. But when we lost Bo, we had no chance. Bo could make players feel as if they were unbeatable. He had this way of making us believe we were always the best team on the field. At Michigan, it was just a given that we were better conditioned and better prepared than any team we would face.

Could his play calling have made a difference? I believe it would have made a difference. One of Bo's strengths as a coach was his ability to assess what was happening on the field. He saw gaps and weaknesses in defensive coverage that we didn't always see. He could sense when someone was breaking down on the other side.

If Bo had been healthy enough to coach on January 1, 1970, I believe that we would have defeated USC.

CHAPTER 3

I QUIT ON BO, BUT HE DIDN'T QUIT ON ME

AS DEAR AS THE UNIVERSITY OF MICHIGAN is now to my heart, it is disconcerting to remember that I actually attempted to walk away from the school and Coach Bo Schembechler in the spring of my sophomore year.

Heading into spring practice, I believed I had proven myself as Michigan's primary tailback. Although I had rushed for 864 yards as a sophomore, my best statistical distinction was my average of 6.1 yards per carry. This was in the era of Bo's three-yards-and-a-cloud-of-dust offense, and my average-per-carry statistic was the kind of number that caught Bo's attention.

My woes started at the beginning of spring practice when I came down with tonsillitis, an illness that bothered me annually since I was a youngster. If you looked in my mouth, it was like looking through a kaleidoscope. My tonsils turned every color in the spectrum. Doctors would tell me that they looked "nasty." The Michigan trainer Lindsey McLean told Bo that I couldn't practice. However, I had witnessed how Bo had pushed everyone mercilessly in fall practice and I didn't want to lose my job. So I decided to keep practicing. I certainly had the impression that Bo expected me to keep practicing. He did not stop me. Even the doctor suggested that I should skip practices in the name of getting well, but I kept participating.

I discovered that in Bo's book, showing up for practice wasn't the same as performing well at practice. At some point during the spring practice period, Bo was quoted in the newspaper as saying that I had not shown him "anything since the Ohio State game."

Today, and even a year after that, I would have known that it was just Bo's way of keeping me hungry, or keeping me focused on trying to improve each week that I was on the field. By the time I was a junior, I understood that as long as Bo was yelling at you, or was unhappy with you, then you were fine. It's when he stopped yelling, that's when you needed to be concerned. That meant he had given up on you. But I was too young and probably too immature to properly analyze Bo's strategy. I wasn't motivated. I was sick. In addition, I was angry, maybe even infuriated.

The next day when it was time after morning classes to meet my roommate Thom Darden for our walk to practice, I made up an excuse about needing to take care of an errand. The night before, I had already decided to transfer out of Michigan. In hindsight, my actions look childish. At the time, it felt as if I was thinking the matter through.

When Darden and the other players were well on their way to practice, I loaded up my car and headed toward Barberton.

When I arrived home, Momma, who still wasn't a huge fan of football because she was always worried about my safety, was supportive of my decision, although she grilled me about what kind of contingency plan I had for assuring I would have a good future.

"Don't worry, Momma," I said, "I've decided to go to Kent State."

By that time, my former Barberton High School Coach Tom "Red" Phillips was the offensive line coach for the Golden Flashes' program. My thinking was that if I called Coach Phillips he would surely welcome me enthusiastically to his program.

Kent State had been a 5-5 team in 1969, but the team boasted a fire hydrant-sized running back named Don Nottingham, who would eventually end up playing in the NFL for the Baltimore Colts and Miami Dolphins. He was heading into his senior season in 1970. Even if I sat out a year, I could have two full seasons as a featured back at Kent State. Nottingham believed he could go from Kent State to the NFL. Certainly that meant I could as well.

I was serious enough about this idea that I went down to watch Kent State's spring practice. To coach Phillips' credit, he was thinking more about what was best for me than he was about his team.

"We would love to have you here at Kent State, but are you sure this is what you want to do?" he asked. "Have you talked to the Michigan coaches? You had better be really sure you know what you are doing, because you are leaving a terrific program."

By then, Michigan assistant coaches Jerry Hanlon and Chuck Stobart were calling me regularly. I had become close to the mom of Billy Harris, a wide receiver who graduated in 1968. She called me and basically told me that I needed to return to Ann Arbor. I don't recall whether Bo called me directly. But the Mellow Men were calling. I specifically remember Darden, Glenn Doughty and Reggie McKenzie making strong pitches to get me to return. "We are Mellow Men,' Darden said. "We said we were going to stick together. We are going to win a championship together."

Another important mentor during that period was Sam Carpenter, father of Butch Carpenter. Early on, he seemed to sense that I needed more guidance than the other members of the Mellow Men who had fathers in their lives.

He called me, and was quite direct: "BT, you have to think about what you are doing. You have to come back. It's important for a man to finish what he starts."

He also reminded me that I was a member of the Mellow Men and I had an obligation to those men. Really, we had made a covenant to be there for each other and I was breaking that covenant.

His words had a profound impact on my thinking. I realized that I was letting a lot of people down, including Bo, the Mellow Men, my teammates, my friends and even my mother. She wanted me to have a Michigan education because she had believed it would lead to me having "a good job."

It was quite clear that I had made a serious mistake. I had failed to rely on the wisdom of my friends and mentors, an error that I would repeat a few years later. Then the consequences would be cataclysmic on my life.

Before I left Ann Arbor, I wish I had remembered the words that my great-grandmother, a former slave, had handed down through the generations.

Apparently my great-grandmother used to say, "Don't go too far, don't stay too long." That credo was passed to her daughter, who had taught that to my mother. She, in turn, taught that to her children. In essence, it meant that a person should live within certain boundaries and limitations. You should never get too carried away with the options that were available to you. You shouldn't stray too far from your friends and family. Temperance in all things, control and limits, do the right things, don't get too carried away. And if you do stray, don't press your luck. Always get back as quickly as you can to your circle of comfort. "Temperance in all things," is another way Momma used to put it.

So many times in my life, I wish I would have embraced those precepts, however, I was able to dig myself out of trouble in this particular instance. I called the assistant coaches to find out what my options were. They informed me that if I returned immediately and made sure I caught up on my schooling, I would keep my scholarship and my place on the team, although I suspected that I would have to prove myself again as a starter. Bo couldn't let me waltz back without any penalty for my actions. It couldn't be swept under the rug. If there were no consequences for poor decisions, there would be no discipline on the team. I understood and respected that notion.

Bo never called me, but I knew he had made the decision to allow me to return. No forgiveness of this magnitude would have been offered unless Bo had authorized it. I was fortunate that Bo looked after me. I know that not every player would have been welcomed back had they walked away from the school. I always suspected Bo frequently gave me the benefit of the doubt because he knew that I had not had a father figure in my life, someone who could have counseled me at times when I was making poor decisions. Can you imagine how my life would have been altered had I left Michigan? The leadership, mentoring and coaching I received as a Michigan Wolverine prepared me for the rest of my life.

As tough as Bo could be on me, he usually ended up being my guardian angel. In 1975, when I got myself in so much legal trouble, it would have been easy for everyone to walk away from me. Bo is as tough as an old grizzly bear, and yet he can show the compassion of Mother Theresa. But I'm not the only player that Bo looked after during his career. Darden tells me that some players believed that I was "receiving special treatment."

I'm proud and thankful—not embarrassed—that he seemed to pay special attention to me. If I did receive some special consideration, I believe that Bo gave it to me because he thought I needed it. If you were in a war, you would want Bo as your general because he would deeply care about his men while he was winning the battles.

Darden does like to joke with Bo about me. "Bo, you support Billy Taylor so much you ought to claim him on your income tax," Darden said to him once.

CHAPTER 4

TOUCHDOWN BILLY TAYLOR
TOUCHDOWN BILLY TAYLOR

WHEN PRESIDENT ABRAHAM LINCOLN WAS asked how long a man's legs should be, his answer was "long enough to reach the ground." When people ask me how fast I was coming out of the Michigan backfield, I answered "as fast as I needed to be."

No one would be able to produce a film showing me getting caught from behind in middle school, high school or my college career.

My best time was 4.56 seconds for 40 yards in full gear. That's about the same time I could run in shorts and cleats. The extra weight of helmet and pads just didn't make a bit of difference. I was a strong runner with big powerful thighs. On more than one occasion, I would break away from speedy defensive backs who supposedly could run a 4.2 or 4.3 for 40 yards. Some of these faster players were skinny guys who could look dazzling in a head-to-head race on the track. But when I was exploding off Reggie McKenzie's turn-up block, I didn't think anyone could beat me to the corner flag. If I saw open field between the goal line and me, you were not going to catch me.

Coach Bo Schembechler used to say that he never had a back that accelerated as quickly as I did out of a standstill. "Taylor," Bo would say, "in your third step you are in full stride."

Back when I was a young man, the guys in the neighborhood would joke that I always ran "like I stole something."

Truthfully, I think I developed some of my quickness by chasing down those rabbits when I worked on the farm in Hartville, Ohio. Those rabbits would dart every which way, but I caught many of them. In the first two or three minutes, the rabbits would elude me, but eventually they would wear down and I would pounce. That clearly helped my agility.

Basically, my objective as a college running back was to gain yardage. My job was to move the chains, to keep us advancing down the field. I had pride in my work. Every game I wanted to prove that I was the best back on the field on either team.

Before I drove to Michigan for my freshman year, I can remember my brother Jim telling me: "Bill, we love you, and we have always supported you, but they have a lot of big guys and a lot of fast guys up there. The competition is going to be tougher than it has ever been."

He paused before continuing, "What I'm saying is that if you don't play or don't play a lot, we still love you. The family will still support you no matter what happens."

This was obviously difficult for my brother to say. He was just trying to say that my value as a person shouldn't be tied to my athletic performance. He didn't want me to feel any pressure. That was certainly something our mom believed. They were truthfully the right words to say to me.

"Thank you very much, Jim," I said, "But I'm going to Michigan and I'm going to turn it out."

I used those exact words. When I started playing at the University of Michigan, I went on the field believing I was going to leave the school as the school's all-time leading ground gainer.

Going into my junior season, Schembechler had decided he wanted to use both Doughty and me in the same backfield. Dependable fullback Garvie Craw had graduated, and Bo decided I would switch to that position, although I was going to get the ball more than Craw did. Garvie was going to be the blocking fullback who occasionally ran with the football. I was going to be a running fullback who occasionally would be a blocking back. Schembechler called Doughty and me into his office and detailed the plan and we were both on board. The plan made plenty of sense. As a sophomore, Doughty had run for 762 yards in 150 carries. That's an average of almost five yards per attempt. His sophomore heroics included three 100-yard games, plus the 80-yard touchdown run in his first varsity game.

As a sophomore, I had gained 864 yards on 141 rushing attempts for a 6.1 yards-per-carry average with touchdown runs of 84, 51, and 71 yards with one 200-yard game and three 100-yard games.

If Doughty and I could mesh together and both improve at the same level, I think Bo thought he could have one of the most productive backfield tandems in the country.

However, the new backfield look didn't function as splendidly as we had planned. Doughty was coming off knee surgery and I didn't seem to run as effectively out of the fullback position. We won our first three games, but we scored only 51 points total against Arizona, Washington and Texas A & M. By Game 4 against Purdue, Bo had moved me back to tailback. I ran for 89 yards against Purdue after never hitting 70 in any of three previous outings in that season. More importantly, my yards-per-carry average rose significantly after returning to tailback.

Unfortunately, in the Purdue contest, I suffered a knee injury that hampered me the rest of the season. As I recall, it was a helmet to knee contact that caused the injury. After the play was whistled down, I remember putting my legs under me to push myself back up after the tackle and my left knee buckled. I had to be helped off the field.

Trainer Lindsey McLean examined the rapidly swelling knee, and he told Bo, "It doesn't look good."

That's not what you want to hear when you are a starting tailback. McLean put ice on the knee to minimize the swelling. After a few minutes, I could put weight on it. I demonstrated some flexibility. Lindsey decided to put a tight wrap on it. I was able to re-enter the game and play on it.

The following Monday doctors diagnosed the injury as a torn medial collateral ligament on the outside of the knee. Surgery was necessary, but the doctors and I felt that I could probably finish the season. The surgery would come in December. It was explained to me that I was going to have to endure daily aggravation to play on a damaged knee. I was willing to do that, although I probably didn't comprehend the full extent of that commitment.

Honestly, I'm not sure any of us really knew whether I could pull this off. I can remember the next week Bo watched me carefully as he went through the drills, making the cuts that I would have to make on the injured knee.

The knee swelled grotesquely after every game and I needed to have it drained every Thursday in preparation for the game. I had to essentially stay off my knee until game time on Saturday. I didn't even participate in the walk-through practice in shorts and helmet on Friday. I would just watch. But I was proud that I was able to finish the season and gain 911 yards.

My willingness to accept some pain in the name of playing and winning put me in a position to challenge Johnson's career yardage record during my senior year. By then, I had a decent bond with Johnson. I had actually visited him when he was playing for the New York Giants over the next couple of years. I even got to meet his quarterback Fran Tarkenton who was a nice man.

Before my senior season, Johnson had given me a pair of Adidas with gold wings on the side. The Giants had given Johnson those shoes. Players started calling me "Billy Blue Suede." I told my teammates, "I'm going to break Ron Johnson's career rushing record wearing these shoes."

As tough as Bo was, he could surprise you by respecting your decisions from time to time. Once you had gotten to know Bo and proven yourself to him, he would allow you to explore some individuality like he did for me when I showed up my senior season wearing those blue suede cleats.

On Bo's team, every player was supposed to wear the same color cleats. On the opening day of the 1971 fall practice, my shoes were blue and everyone else was wearing black.

"What the hell are these pansy shoes doing on your feet?" Bo bellowed.

"Bo," I replied, "I'm going to run for 100 or more yards per game this season, but I need to wear these shoes. Just let me wear these shoes."

Bo didn't like non-conformity, but he wasn't as rigid as some people think. He allowed me to wear the shoes. In return, I made sure I fulfilled my side of the bargain. Entering my senior season, I needed 665 yards to break Johnson's mark of 2,440 yards, established from 1966-1968. If I could stay healthy, the projection was that I would break the record mid-season. After back-to-back games of 100 yards against Michigan State and Illinois, I needed just 85 yards on the road against Minnesota to break the record. I managed to run for 88 yards just in the first half. I was wearing Johnson's shoes when I broke the record.

In my senior season, I rushed for more than 100 yards in 6 of my 11 games, and gained 90 yards in three others. I never rushed for fewer than 76 yards in any game and I surpassed Johnson's career yardage total by more than 600 yards.

After the record was broken, teammates congratulated me and even Bo walked away from his game management just a few seconds to pass along his form of a pat on the back.

"Good job Taylor, but we still got a game to win," Schembechler said.

That was high praise indeed coming from the general. He didn't dispense compliments with any regularity. During my three seasons at Michigan, the words I heard most often from Coach Bo Schembechler was, "Taylor, you are the worst damn back I ever coached."

After a while, it almost becomes comforting to have Bo grumbling at you. It's sort of a reminder of how much he still cares. Even in the midst of my third All-American season, Bo didn't soften his rhetoric. Once when I broke four or five tackles on a 10-yard touchdown run, I went back to the sideline and Bo screamed at me, "Hot damn, Taylor, get the truck off your back. You are running like a sissy." Nevertheless, I loved that man.

His approach was old school. He commanded his team as if he was General George Patton. In fact, we would often refer to him privately as "Patton." Bo would often use military analogies, saying we were close because we had been "in the battles together." He also liked to challenge your manhood. He wasn't afraid to call you a "ham and egger" if he didn't think you were playing manly enough. He pushed his players to their breaking points. But deep down you always believed he loved his players. He was always partial to seniors, and the presumption was that Bo simply knew that experience was a key factor in determining the outcome of college football games. However, I think Bo liked seniors because he treasured loyalty. He knew that the players who had made it through their senior year were loyal to him and he was loyal to them.

After one game when Bo cussed at me even more than usual, Mellow Man linebacker Mike Taylor told me that when I was running the ball on a long gainer Bo would be screaming, "Go Bill, go Bill, that's showing them how to run the football."

The funny aspect of that story was that when I came off the field after that lengthy jaunt, Bo had yelled at me: "Damn Taylor, get in shape."

The day after I became Michigan's all-time leading rusher, the classy Johnson called me to congratulate me. It was fitting that I broke the record against Minnesota because I tore up the Gophers. As

Billy Taylor at 3 months of age in Hoxie, Arkansas.

Future legend B.T. at age 11 while a student at U. L. Light Junior High School in Barberton, Ohio.

Aunt Hattie Wells in Arkansas during the early 1950s. She had a profound influence on B.T.'s childhood.

Uncle Eugene Wells in Arkansas during the early 1950s.

Biological mother Mariah Marie Taylor. Photo taken just prior to B.T.'s 1972 trip to the Rose Bowl. She often worried Billy would get hurt while playing football.

Dr. Billy Taylor's mother's birthplace, Mound Bayou, Mississippi. This is the first African American township established after the Civil War.

5th grade basketball team at Washington Elementary School in Barberton, Ohio. Billy Taylor is in the 1st row, 2nd from the right side.

This house now sits on the original site of Dr. Billy Taylor's birthplace in Hoxie, Arkansas.

Dr. Billy Taylor entering his place of birth, Hoxie, Arkansas after a 54 year absence.

Son William Taylor, daughter Mariah and Dr. Taylor with B.T.'s middle school coach, David Robinson, while visiting Robinson's home.

B.T.'s precious gifts from God. Children: Clockwise from left: Mariah, William, Mariah, Alden, and William.

Dr. Taylor and his sons William and Alden sharing some good times in downtown Detroit during the early 1980s.

Taylor family Christmas, 2001 reuniting with children Alden, Mariah, and William after a long absence.

Having some fun and creating precious memories with children, L-R Alden, Billy holding Mariah, and William during Christmas in Detroit, 2002.

Dr. Taylor with baseball star and namesake William Taylor III after a ball game at Mumford High School, Detroit.

William Taylor III, Mumford High School graduation photo.

Dr. Taylor with daughter Mariah. She inherited his magnetic personality.

B.T. proud to be with his kids while at Sheryl Carson's Family Tyes, Detroit, 1998.

Proud of son Alden at his ceremony after graduating from Cass Tech High School in Detroit.

Oldest son Lewis Askew in Akron, Ohio.

Heartwarming reunion after seven years with oldest brother Felix Ware, a retired army officer in San Diego, 2002.

Nephew Harry Davis of Aliquippa, Pennsylvania.

Dr. Billy Taylor with his older brothers, the late Thomas "Jack" Jackson and James during 1998 New Year's celebration.

Cousin Dorothy Thomas, sister Lucille Lewis, Dr. Billy Taylor and sister Clara Bingham at Clara's home in Akron, Ohio in the summer of 2002. A special bond still exists between them today.

Niece Rhonda with brothers Tom and James Jackson during New Years 1998, Akron, Ohio.

Nephew Calvin Davis, Dr. Billy Taylor and nephew Reverend Clarence Davis at sister Juanita's home in Aliquippa, Pennsylvania (Christmas 2002).

With Niece Marie Davis during New Years in 2004 in Aliquippa, Pennsylvania.

With Cousins Marlene Chutes and Lori Brown in Columbus, Ohio (Christmas 2003).

First cousin Helen Wells and daughter Sandra in Cleveland (Christmas 2003).

With cousin Jessica Ellis in Columbus, Ohio (Christmas 2003).

Brother Felix Ware, his daughter
Barbara and son Randy at Barbara's
wedding in Las Vegas, 1999.

Cousin Jessica "Bibbs" Ellis
and husband Willard (Columbus, Ohio 2003).

Sister Juanita Davis and her husband
Lugene in Aliquippa, Pennsylvania.

Taylor with his "sis" Sheryl Carson
on vacation in Lake Tahoe, Nevada.

Dr. Billy Taylor's mother, Marie Polk
and "sis" Sheryl Carson on vacation in
Los Angeles (summer 2003).

Dr. Taylor's family: "sis" Sheryl Carson,
mother Marie Polk, grandmother Annis
Benjamin, friend Veronica, and sister
Paula at a family dinner in Detroit (fall
2003).

Taylor's "sis" Sheryl Carson and mother Marie Polk shopping in Detroit (fall 2003).

With "sis" Sheryl Carson on vacation with family and friends at Lake Tahoe (August 1998).

Dr. Billy Taylor with sister Sheryl Carson (summer 1997).

On the road, the Taylor family with bus driver friend at the home of Buffalo Bill Cody. (summer 1998).

Mother Marie Polk and cousin Benny enjoying vacation spots in San Francisco (summer 1998).

Clowning around with daughter Mariah and "sis" Sheryl Carson at Family Tyes (summer 1998).

Sister Juanita Davis and niece Marie Davis visit Billy Taylor while at Family Tyes.

Brother Jim Jackson and his wife Helen.

Sister-in-law Helen Jackson, and Nieces Valeria and Erica.

With nieces Diedra and Crystal at "sis" Sheryl's home in West Bloomfield, Michigan.

Extended family members and former Wolverine Brian Carpenter with his mother Arie Carpenter and her grandchild Alden. (She is the mother of former Wolverine the late Alden "Butch" Carpenter.)

Lifelong friends from Barberton, Ohio: Bill Von Stein and sons.

Outside of the Ebenezer Baptist Church in Atlanta, Georgia (summer 2003). God continues to guide Taylor in the right direction.

Standing in front of The Southern Christian Leadership Conference in Atlanta, Georgia. (summer 2003.) Today, Dr. Taylor presents his message of hope and racial tolerance as a leading speaker at venues across America.

On holiday at Windsor Castle in Windsor, England (November 11, 2004). Inspiration can arise from any place at any time.

A visit to the birthplace of Shakespeare, Stratford-on-Avon, England (November 2004).

Continuing his quest to learn as much about the civil rights icon as he can, Dr. Taylor visits Dr. Martin Luther King's birthplace on Auburn St. in Atlanta, Georgia. Dr. Martin Luther King is truly one of the world's greatest citizens.

Dr. Taylor feels the presence of his personal hero, Dr. Martin Luther King, near King's gravesite in Atlanta, Georgia during a summer sojourn in 2003.

In London at the West End Theater District (November 11, 2004).

Dr. Taylor contemplates one of the world's most intriguing mysteries while admiring Stonehenge in England. (November 11, 2004.)

Power, speed, explosiveness, quick thinking, outstanding teammates and God-given athletic genius propelled Billy Taylor to the pantheon of college footballs greatest players. (Photo by Bob Kalmbach, courtesy of The Bentley Historical Library, University of Michigan.)

November 1, 1969: Michigan vs. Wisconsin, Billy Taylor exploded for 142 yards. Teammates #81, Mike Hankwitz, #48 Garvie Craw, #60 Bob Baumgartner and #53 Guy Murdock clear the way for #42.

1972 Rose Bowl: Bo Schembechler and Billy Taylor accepting the ceremonial flower from the Rose Bowl Queen, Margo Lynn.

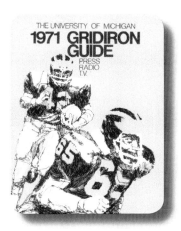

1971 Media guide cover featuring Billy Taylor and fellow superstar Reggie McKenzie.

Mike Taylor and Billy Taylor enjoying star status on the cover of The Gridiron.

OSU 1969 program. Pictured L-R are Fritz Crisler, Bennie Oosterbaan, Bump Elliott and coach Bo.

Star teammates B.T., Fred Grambau, Reggie McKenzie, Ed Shuttlesworth, Frank Gusich and Glenn Doughty.

As Sport Magazines's College Athlete of the Month, senior tailback Billy Taylor traveled to the White House to meet President Nixon.

125 year All-Class Reunion in "The Big House." L-R Chalmers "Bump" Elliott, Bo Schembechler, Dr. Billy Taylor, Gary Moeller, and Lloyd Carr.

Michigan vs. Ohio State. Billy Taylor celebrates after his famous game winning touchdown.

Fellow Wolverine teammates #99 Tom Beckman and #94 Al "Butch" Carpenter.

As a sophomore, Billy Taylor helped his team reach new heights.

Touchdown Billy Taylor! Fellow teammates #13 Larry Cipa and #32 Fritz Seyferth run interference as Taylor drives to the endzone to score his legendary winning touchdown against Ohio State University in 1971 to defeat the Buckeyes.
(Photo by Bob Kalmbach, courtesy of The Bentley Historical Library, University of Michigan.)

125 year All-Class Reunion, June
2004. Dr. Billy Taylor with Charles
Woodson (Michigan Wolverine,
Oakland Raider, and Heisman Trophy
winner.) (Photo by Phillip F of Detroit.)

Reminiscing with "brother" Brian
Carpenter a former Wolverine,
Washington Redskin and Super
Bowl star.

Former Michigan Coach
Jerry Hammond.

Dr. Billy Taylor, Bo Schembechler,
and Son William Taylor.

Former teammates Larry Cipa and
Lonnie Taylor.

The Mayor of Las Vegas, Oscar
Goodman, greets Dr. Billy Taylor
in Las Vegas, Nevada.

Former Community College of Southern
Nevada President Ron Remington and CCSN
Athletic Director, Tim Chambers.

Retired University of Las Vegas Nevada, Hall of Fame coach
Jerry Tarkanian, and his son Coach
George Tarkanian of the Community College of Southern Nevada.

Former teammate,
linebacker Tom Key.

U of M standouts and two of the
"Mellow Men": Mike Taylor and Dr.
Billy Taylor at University of Michigan reunion.

Former roommates and teammates:
Mike Taylor, Reggie McKenzie, and
Bo Rather.

All-Star teammate, former
defensive end, Cecil Prior.

With friends and former Wolverine
brothers, Reggie McKenzie and Fred
Grambeau, celebrating 125 years of
Michigan football.

Allan "Cowboy" Walker, Bo Schembechler, and Dr. Billy Taylor relish their
greateat Michigan seasons.

Shown at age 50, B.T. looks like he could still razzle dazzle on the field. His daily regimen includes healthy eating habits and multiple vitamins.

Dr. Billy Taylor: mentor, life coach, and gifted motivational speaker en route to one of his many uplifting appearances.

Traveling to Atlanta to visit his oldest son Lewis Askew. The future is looking bright.

Spending quality time with oldest son Lewis Askew, (R) and his friend Charles Parker, in Decatur, Georgia (summer 2002).

Reunites in Las Vegas with the Godfather of Soul in the summer of 2004. B.T. first met James Brown during his senior year of high school.

Dr. Billy Taylor "sitting in" with the Music Town MVP's Jim King (keyboards and vocals), Dick Fidge (lead vocals) and Bob Resch (drums and percussion) at the Ypsilanti recording studio. Produced by Immortal Investments Publishing and Music Town Productions, Billy contributed vocals and helped to co-write his theme song "Get Back Up" which chronicles his life and times.

a sophomore, I had rushed for 151 yards and three touchdowns during a 35-9 victory in Minneapolis. As a junior, I gained 151 yards and scored once. In my senior game against the Gophers, I finished with 166 yards and two touchdowns to help us down Minnesota 31-7 to preserve our No. 3 national ranking. "It was just like homecoming for me," I told the press after the game. In my three games against Minnesota during my career, I finished with 468 yards rushing and six TDs.

A week later, I rolled for 172 yards against Indiana. By the end of the season, I had established 3,072 yards as the new school record for rushing yards in a career.

The following season, the NCAA changed the rule to allow freshmen to be eligible, which meant my record wasn't going to stand for long. Rob Lytle played as a freshman in 1973, and by 1976, he had broken my mark by more than 200 yards. Five years after Lytle was gone, Butch Woolfolk broke his record by more than 500 yards.

However, the school record I still hold today is the mark of 102.4 yards per game. I'm the only tailback in Michigan history to average 100 yards per game and I'm proud of that distinction. Everyone in front of me on the all-time list played more than 40 games. I played in exactly 30 games at Michigan. Anthony Thomas rushed for 4,472 yards in his career, but he played in 49 games.

Also in Bo's early years we were stacked with running backs, and Schembechler liked to use a stable of fresh backs. While I was at Michigan, we had Doughty, Preston Henry, Alan "Cowboy" Walker and two or three others competing for playing time. We had had five guys who could have played starting tailback at other Big Ten schools. Out of the 30 games I played, I bet I only played three full games. Usually by the start of the third quarter, Bo was looking to put me on the shelf. In the second half, Bo would be using Doughty or Walker.

* * *

By my senior season, I believe I had matured into the running back that Bo wanted me to be. Although I was still not the country's best blocker, I had improved considerably in that area. My strength was that I was explosive going into and coming out of the hole, and I could carry would-be tacklers. One day, Bo said in the newspaper he wanted his backs focused on "getting the first down yardage" as they burst through the line and not looking all around trying to find a seam to break the long gainer. Bo believed that if you were focused on the first downs, then the long gainers would come as a result of that. That's the kind of back I became at Michigan. I liked to believe that in 1971 I could match-up with any back in the country.

I had gained some notoriety—some of it serious and some of it funny. *Sport Magazine* named me college player of the month, which meant I would get a trip to the White House to meet President Nixon. But one of my amusing moments of notoriety came in a case of mistaken identity.

During my senior year, I was in Chicago staying at the Hilton when a group of youngsters came running toward me, with pen and paper gripped tightly in their hands. Obviously, they had seen a face they recognized and pieced together who I was.

"Joe, Joe, Joe—will you give us your autograph?" they shouted. "Who's Joe?" I asked. "You are," they said. "You're Joe Frazier." I laughed hard, although later on I joked that I was actually insulted because I didn't think the heavyweight boxing champion Frazier "was very cute."

The most memorable play of my Wolverines' career, the one that defined my three varsity seasons, came on my last offensive play at Michigan Stadium in 1971. It was against Ohio State. Trailing the entire game, we took over the ball deep in our own territory with several minutes remaining. Just before the offensive unit went on the field, Bo gathered his players together and said, "This could be our last possession, and we want first down after first down and we aren't stopping until we get the touchdown."

Bo was animated, overflowing with purpose and passion. He was like a preacher, telling his congregation that it was time to rise up and do what you were born to do. He said it was time for the seniors to take charge. That's exactly what the seniors did. I was one of those seniors and Bo had always sermonized that seniors had to step up and make the impact plays. That was the essence of Bo's football philosophy. Sophomores and juniors were like apprentices, learning how to become skilled football players. As underclassmen, you could be significant contributors, but you weren't really master craftsmen quite yet. Once you became a senior, you were expected to lead others and be a difference maker. Bo leaned heavily on his seniors because he believed that experience ruled in close games.

I remember the events like they occurred yesterday. Many people remember my run, but they forget that before my TD gallop we were faced with a fourth-and-one situation. The unsung hero on that drive was fullback Fritz Seyferth who never received enough credit for his contributions. He only rushed for 529 yards in his career, but some of the yards came in the most difficult circumstances. When we needed one inch for a first down, Fritz could get you two inches and when you needed three inches, he could get you four. He had 12 touchdowns in his career, including a four-touchdown game against Minnesota in our junior season. When Fritz wasn't gaining a tough yard, he was creating large holes for me. He was a devastating blocker, and he had enough skill that he was able to play for the Calgary Stampeders in the Canadian Football League after his college career was complete. He could clear a path like a lumberjack clearing a forest. He would topple defenders one right after another.

The best man to describe the events of those closing minutes is the late Michigan radio broadcaster Bob Ufer whose calls of Michigan football games are now legendary. I have a tape of his call, starting with the fourth-and-one situation. Here is how Ufer described the action:

"Cipa under center, gives the ball to Seyferth and Seyferth's got it. The determined senior that he is... needed a yard and he got it to the 21-yard line. Two minutes and 34 seconds remaining. That's an automatic timeout for a first down." Billy Taylor is down to the 20, down to 15, down to 10, 5, 4, 3, 2, 1. Touchdown Billy Taylor,

Touchdown Billy Taylor. Billy Taylor scores a touchdown from 21 yards out. The crowd is going berserk. Michigan leads 9-7."

Old man Ufer has been broadcasting for 27 years and I have never seen anything like this. Thirty-two years ago in 1939 Ohio State led Michigan and the Wolverines came back in the last 27 seconds to beat Ohio State 21-14. Thirty-two years later, Michigan trailing with two minutes remaining 7-3 come back up field and they march 80 yards and they have gone into the Buckeyes endzone for the first time this afternoon. Believe me...my eyes...I'm an old man. I have maize and blue spots in front of me right now.

Even without the help of Ufer's passionate call, I have vivid memories of that play. When we broke huddle, someone said, "Everyone on their blocks, *everyone* on their blocks." I told myself that I was going to score. I told myself I would not be brought down. When the ball was pitched, it was almost like slow motion. I could see our line cracking. Bo Rather made a crackback block and I saw a guy flipping. Seyferth was leading me around the corner. There were about four people in front of me. There was one defender with a true shot at me but Fritz rubbed him out like he had done a 100 times before. Another Buckeye guy came out of nowhere but I outran him. I went into the end zone untouched for the winning score. That gave us an undefeated regular season and a Rose Bowl bid.

It was an unforgettable scene in Ann Arbor as we celebrated. The game will also be remembered for a temper tantrum Ohio State Coach Woody Hayes threw on the sideline. Probably Momma's instincts about him were on the mark. He probably wasn't the right coach for me.

After I had scored, the Buckeyes mounted an effort to rally. It was snuffed out by Mellow Man Thom Darden's interception with just over a minute remaining. My man Darden out-wrestled receiver Dick Wakefield for the ball. Woody had been miffed about the officiating for much of the day. After the play, Woody stormed on to the field, screaming that interference should have been called. The officials tagged Woody with an unsportsmanlike conduct penalty.

Meanwhile, Woody was escorted off the field by some of his players. He almost got into a fight with one of them. It was a crazy scene.

I finished that game with 118 yards on the ground and Bo gave me the game ball. Everyone was clapping, and I raised my hand to stop them. I wanted the floor.

"I'm honored to receive this game ball but I believe it should be given to quarterback Larry Cipa," I told everyone.

Cipa, out of Cincinnati, Ohio, was really a sophomore third-string quarterback and he had stepped into the game and made the perfect pitch that set-up the "Touchdown, Billy Taylor" run. It was a pressure-filled situation. Our perfect regular-season and Big Ten championship was on the line.

My thinking was that most of the key players were seniors who knew what it took to get the job done. Bo used to make it a point to remind us that seniors are supposed to rise up and make whatever big move is required to make the play. All of the seniors believed it was their job to deliver the victory, and here was this sophomore who hadn't played much, executing a perfectly timed pitch with the game on the line. In my mind, I was doing what was expected of me and he had exceeded expectations. I wanted him to have the ball.

Cipa had stepped up to the line with authority and barked his signals confidently. There was no fear in him. It was a flawless play. You couldn't have drawn it any better on the board. Cipa faked the handoff well enough to suck in the defensive end. I also remember that after Cipa made the pitch, he hustled up to the line of scrimmage and threw a block.

Bo told me afterward that he was proud of me for presenting my game ball to Cipa. "Bill, that was unselfish," Bo told me. "That's what a team is all about."

My mother was at that game, and she was at the Den of the Mellow Men with all of the other parents after that game. You could hear the pride in everyone's voices that night and see it in their faces. We were celebrating, but I also think there was a hint of sadness in there because we knew that our group wouldn't be together much longer. We were going to graduate and play in the NFL. We would be scattered in different directions. The Mellow Men were family, and it was hard to think about breaking up the family dynamic. I believe my mother was very proud of me—not just because of what I had done on the field. I believe she was proud of the man I had grown into. Likewise, I think all of the parents were proud of the Mellow Men.

Mr. Carpenter had been right. We were a special group. We had made history. Michigan was 11-0 after that game, and this marked the first time the team had won all its regular-season games since 1948. The Wolverines were ranked No. 3 in the country after that game, but we believed we were capable of beating any team in the country.

In the three seasons that the Mellow Men played varsity, Michigan won 28 football games and two Big Ten Championships.

I finished the season with 1,297 yards, which was 97 yards shy of Johnson's single-season record. We were heading to the Rose Bowl, and then I had been invited to play in a senior All-Star game—the All-American Bowl in Tampa, Florida. The NFL draft was scheduled for February 1 and I believed I had proven myself to the point that NFL teams would be lining up for my services. I had plans for my NFL earnings. I was going to buy my mother a new house with all the furnishings. To be honest, that prospect excited me even more than the thought of wearing a NFL uniform.

My experience at the university was probably the most important experience of my life and I'm proud as a peacock that I went there. The lessons I learned as a Michigan Wolverine prepared me for life. Bo, Bump and teammates taught me never to give up, even when the odds were against you. If you are knocked down, get back up. That was *the Michigan way*. Those lessons would become more valuable later in life.

The good folks in Barberton had taken up a collection to pay for my mother to make the trip to the Rose Bowl to watch her son play his final collegiate game.

I was also on schedule to receive my degree in four years. Remember, I was only the third member of my family to graduate from high school. Jimmy and Juanita were the other two siblings to graduate from high school. My life seemed to be going the way I wanted it to go at that point. It was close to perfect. It seemed as if I was headed toward the good life that I had always desired. I didn't see my derailment coming.

CHAPTER 5

LOSING MY RELIGION

MARIAH MARIE TAYLOR WAS A PERSON who could foresee the rainbow even as she was enduring the thunderstorm. She believed in the goodness of God even on the gloomiest of days. My mother was the peacemaker in all conflicts great and small. She could find the best in people even at the worst of times.

One of the most vivid memories I have of my mother is her standing outside the gate waiting for me after the Rose Bowl on the late afternoon of New Year's Day of 1972. I was already in a foul mood because we had lost to Stanford 13-12 on a 31-yard field goal by Rod Garcia with 16 seconds left in the game. However, I was even more upset when Momma told me that my sister-in-law Mary had upset her with some non-Christian behavior, including the use of profanity, in my mother's presence. Everyone in my family was respectful of Momma's beliefs. We all tried to hold our tongues around her because we loved her so deeply. But my brother Felix's wife, Mary, had a tendency to be boisterous at times, and occasionally rude. Felix and Mary lived in San Diego, and Momma was staying with them while attending the Rose Bowl festivities. I can't remember what the issue was, but the loudness upset Momma. Her verbiage stung my mother. I was quite angry.

As was her nature, Momma worked her charm to bring peace to the situation. As upset as she was by what had transpired at Felix's home, she became quite determined to make sure the problem didn't escalate.

"Don't you say anything to Felix because he is your older brother," Momma said. "It's better left alone. It's not going to make it better if you are yelling at Felix." She extracted a promise that the matter would die, and then began to console me about the loss.

"Son, this is just a game," she said. "Michigan has been good to you. You are going to have your degree and you have all of these fine friends. Be thankful to God for all that you have. You will be going down to Florida soon and I'm going to be praying for you."

It was the last time I saw Momma alive.

She was driven to Felix's home in San Diego after the game, and I went out with some of my teammates. Later that night I called her when I returned to my room at the Pasadena Sheraton. She assured me that the situation at Felix's house had been straightened out and she was feeling better about it. I reminded her that I wouldn't be calling her for a couple of days because I would be flying directly to Tampa for the American Bowl, which featured some of college football's best college seniors. Glenn Doughty would be going with me. The following days we would be tied up learning the playbook and practicing.

"You say your prayers," she said to me. "And you know that I will be praying that everything works out for you. I hope you will have a good game."

"I will say my prayers," I said. "And Momma, I love you."

"I love you son," she said. That conversation has been replayed many times in my mind because it was the last one I had with my mother.

On the evening of January 4, I was out eating a steak dinner with Doughty and a few other players when the restaurant manager came around looking for Bill Taylor. I identified myself and he said there was a phone call for me at the cashier's station. When I grabbed the telephone, I heard a very familiar voice on the other end and I started laughing.

"Bo," I said, "How did you find me here?" There was no laughter at his end. "Bill I have some bad news for you," he said. "Your mother has passed away. Your family didn't know how to reach you and they called me."

I fell to my knees on the floor, overwhelmed by my grief. "It can't be true," I said. "It can't be true." The most important person in my life was suddenly gone. My anchor, my guiding force, had been taken away from me. I knew in an instant that I would never again be the same person I was before I had received that call.

Later I found out that Momma had been in the kitchen where she collapsed and died of a heart attack. She died five days before her 62nd birthday. She died three days before my 23rd birthday. Her wake was a day after my birthday and she was buried on January 10.

The next week was a living nightmare, enduring the most catastrophic event of my life. I stayed with my brother Jim and his wife Helen at their home in Akron. I didn't eat for five days. I just drank water. I stayed in my room, listening to *"It's a Family Affair"* by Sly and the Family Stone. I replayed that tune over and over.

When you grow up with no father, is the bond with your mother even stronger? I don't know the answer to that. However, I do know that my mother was my heart and joy. I was as devoted to her welfare, as she was to mine. I was more concerned about her future than I was about my own. She didn't have a retirement plan and I dreamed of making her golden years very comfortable when I was in the NFL.

I like to believe that Momma had a special place in her heart for me because I was the youngest of her seven children, but the truth was Momma was devoted to all of her children.

Everyone in the community loved my mother. My high school coach Red Phillips called her "Mom Taylor." All of the kids in the area called her Mom. We left our door open in Barberton, because no one would do harm to my mom or my family. When people knocked and no one answered, they would leave. At night, we didn't lock the door.

After the funeral I stayed around Akron and Barberton, unable to escape my grief or find relief from my pain. My roommates called and tried to coax me back, but I told the Mellow Men, "To hell with school, to hell with football, to hell with life."

They informed Bo that I was AWOL from campus and he began to look for me.

In my mind, I began to embrace the irrational belief that I would be the next in my family to die. I wasn't suicidal. I never have been suicidal. However, I really believed my life was going to end. I didn't know how. But if someone would have walked up to me on the street and put a gun to my forehead, I would have said: "I've been expecting you." That's just the way I felt. I thought my mom's death was a sign that my life was over. I also began to dwell on the idea that neither my mom nor my Aunt Ernestine Bibbs wanted me to play professional football because they thought it was too closely tied to gambling and gambling was sinful. Wouldn't I be disrespecting my mother's memory if I played in the NFL? This was an idea that circled in my thoughts like a plane in a holding pattern.

At this time in my life, I probably began to open my heart and mind to years of depression. I didn't care about myself, or anyone else for that matter. I fought at the drop of a hat. If you bumped into me, and said "I'm sorry." I would say, "Hell yes you are sorry and I would fire on you." After punching you out, I would say, "You are real sorry now, aren't you?"

The anger in my soul was difficult to contain. I drank. I smoked. I fought. I avoided all of my close friends, and I put myself in isolation. I'm also sorry to say that after my mother died I turned my back on the most important teachings she passed on to her children—the trust in our Lord and Savior.

I began to curse God for the first time in my life. I blamed him for my mother's death.

Although I didn't formally withdraw from class, I didn't attend any classes. I really did believe that I was dropping out of the University of Michigan with less than four months left until graduation.

Somehow, Bo found me. It's like he had Billy Taylor radar. If I had flown to a deserted island in the Pacific, Bo would have tracked me down.

"Bill, you are coming back to school," Bo said, making it sound more like an order than a request. "You are Billy Taylor, All-American, and you aren't going to throw your life away. Your mother would want you to graduate. You need to make your mother proud of you."

That comment pierced my soul. Mariah Marie Taylor would often say, "Lord, I just want one child to go to college and graduate."

Even when I was young, I knew Momma was talking to me when she said that. I knew I had to return to school, but I wasn't going to pursue a professional football career. Regaining my footing academically was like gaining tough yardage. I had to pull several all-nighters to rehabilitate my academic standing. But I graduated in June with my class. In my heart, I dedicated that day to Momma's memory.

Truthfully, graduation didn't heal the wound in my heart. I was still pulling away from friends, and trying unsuccessfully to find some relief from my pain through alcohol. Bo and others were still trying to convince me that I should pursue a professional career. I still had this unshakable feeling that I was going to die. Maybe it was just a premonition of more pain to come.

By fall, I had known struggles in my football career. However, I found joy when I met a lovely woman named Valerie Cole from Belleville, Michigan. In appearance, she looked how I envisioned my mother would have looked as a young woman. I don't know if she was an athlete in high school, but she was physical. She had a fantastically muscular body. She could challenge me at arm wrestling and if she punched me, it would hurt. Valerie looked a bit like a young Natalie Cole.

Coincidentally, Valerie had lived on a farm, with pigs, chickens and ducks. It was a life similar to what my mother had known as a young woman.

When we met, Valerie was married and seeking a divorce. Mostly, we saw each other privately, not wanting to create a public controversy. She was afraid of how her husband would react. However, we were very much in love. We were talking about becoming engaged as soon as her divorce became final. I regret that I never told her specifically that she was the only positive aspect of my life. At that point, I was probably mounting my best fight against depression. I wanted to restore some normalcy to my life. I thought this woman was very special. I thought it was time to settle down, to drink less and work more toward building a family. I wanted to be a father, and I wanted to be there for my children.

One night I was at my Ambassador Arms apartment in Ypsilanti, Michigan waiting for Valerie to come over after roller-skating. That girl loved to skate.

Another phone call—another announcement of tragedy. Valerie was dead. I screamed. I began to throw the telephone, lamps, books and other items across my apartment. I had an Old English Sheep dog named Gray Friar's Duke and he was so fearful of my anger that he hid from me. I threw myself on the bed. I remember sliding on the floor and not getting up for hours. Death was staring at me again. Surely, I thought, I now would be next to die. I couldn't fathom going through another funeral.

The specific details about what happened at the roller rink have been lost in my memory banks. Maybe my mind has thrown them overboard to spare me more pain. However, I know Valerie's cousin was involved in a fight and she had intervened. A gang killed her for that intervention.

At the funeral, I sat by myself. I looked at her husband and I was angry because I thought his sorrow was insincere. He did not love Valerie the way I loved Valerie. Her brothers knew me, and they saw me at the church. They appreciated my pain. I began to cry and I couldn't stop. I remember rising from the pew and exiting the church. I was shaking for an hour.

My emotional collapse gained momentum after Valerie's death. I didn't look to my friends for help. I wasn't the kind of drinker who liked to go to bars and sip beers. I bought a bottle, went to the park, drank by myself, and thought about Momma, Valerie and Uncle Eugene. I wondered if my Uncle Eugene had gone crazy. I wondered if I was going crazy. I wondered when I was going to die. I was sure it would be soon.

Even today, I have a difficult time expressing feelings about Valerie's death. Years ago, I sought refuge in a poem I wrote about Valerie entitled:

THE NIGHT I LOST VALERIE

People screaming and cops all around
Valerie had been stricken down

She got involved trying to break up a fight
And wound up the victim of a kitchen knife

A gang of girls held Valerie tight
While a sixteen year old swung her knife

People yelled a disturbance outside
The officer said it's just another fight

When they came out, Valerie was on the ground
The ones responsible was no where to be found

In my apartment I waited for Valerie
Not knowing death had taken her from me

She said I'll see you tomorrow when we spoke our last
Now more than twenty-four hours have already passed

But now Valerie was lying in a trance
She died in the back of an ambulance

My telephone rang late that night
And I was told there had been a fight

I was *in shock after hearing words like lead*
Her cousin told me that Valerie was dead

She went out that night to a roller-rink
She loved to skate but she didn't like to drink

A kind girl with a simple life
The kind of girl I wanted for my wife

Now she's gone and there's just her memory
And the kind of love I felt for Valerie

Few people know what that did to me
Her life taken so foolishly

There was people screaming and cops all around
That night my Valerie was stricken down

More than 30 years after the death of a mother, aunt, uncle and Valerie, I would say you never really stop grieving. My pain dulled over time, but I will always miss them. When I hear the Spinners' song, "Sadie," I always think about Momma. There is one line that could have been written about her: *"If there's a heaven up above, I know she's teaching angels how to love."*

♫ ♫

Sweeter than cotton candy
Stronger than papas old brandy
Always that needed smile
Once in awhile she would break down and cry
Sometimes she'd be so happy
Just being with us and daddy
Standing the worst of times
Breaking the binds with just a simple song
Oh, Sadie (Oh, Sadie, baby)
Don't you know we love you (She'll love us all in a special way)
Sweet Sadie (Well, well, well)
Place no one above you
Sweet Sadie (Sweet Sadie livin' in the past)

Living in the past
Oh, she's never sinnin'
In love she's always winnin', yeah
Sweet Sadie (How you gave me love, oh, Lord)

CHAPTER 6

UNDERSTANDING AUNT EMMA'S FEAR

AS A HUMAN BEING, YOU ARE INCLINED to remember your first bicycle, your first best friend and your first kiss. As a black person, you are also inclined to remember the first moment you understood racial bigotry.

You may not have realized the impact at the moment of occurrence, but at some point in your life the incident replays often enough in your mind that it becomes clear that it was monumental. Today, I know that my introduction to racism came in 1953 when I was a thirsty four-year-old child walking on the streets of downtown Memphis.

This particular memory involved Aunt Emma and her best friend Miss Pecola who were two of the most colorful characters of my early life in Tennessee. Aunt Emma was my father's sister and Miss Pecola was her best friend. They were two southern black ladies, probably in their mid-60s at the time, who were always resplendent in their buttoned-down, long sleeve dresses, accessorized by white gloves and purses. They never left the house without a hat—not the big, colorful puffy hats that some of the white ladies wore, but the small, dignified, practical hats that I sometimes have seen depicted in movies about Harlem in the 1920s and 1930s. Both Aunt Emma and Miss Pecola liked to drink beer and have just a taste of the corn liquor. They would also like to dip a little snuff, much to the chagrin of my sweet mother.

"Emma," my mother would say, "you shouldn't be drinking all that beer, especially around my baby boy."

Miss Pecola suffered from what everyone called "a nervous condition." Her hands would shake so much that her beer would frequently slosh over the sides of her mug before it ever got to her lips. One day, I was sitting in a chair and she came over to talk to "her honey," as she called me. Her tremor got the best of her, and her beer rained down on me until I was soaked. Momma grabbed me, and I can still hear her saying, "Lord have mercy, you are getting that beer all over this baby."

Aunt Emma and Miss Pecola also loved to go the ballpark to watch the Memphis Red Sox play in the Negro League. I'm sure Momma had reservations about placing her youngster in the care of two ladies whose fondness for spirits was well established. But she allowed me to go.

Both of the ladies were talkers. However, I noticed as soon as we would arrive at the bus stop they would both become more reserved, less chatty, and far more serious.

When the bus would pull up, Aunt Emma would have her tightest grip on my hand. As a four-year-old, I had trouble negotiating the steep stairs leading up to the bus, but it wasn't an issue because Aunt Emma was essentially dragging me up. I'm not sure my feet ever touched any of those steps. Once in the bus, Aunt Emma and Miss Pecola would quick-step march to the back without uttering a word. The two jovial ladies lost their humor as soon as they were on the bus. I noticed that they no longer wanted to play with me when we were aboard that bus. They hushed me if I even tried to open my mouth. When the bus ride was over, they would revert to being the sweet, colorful characters that they were.

It wasn't until I was a few years older that I realized that Aunt Emma and Miss Pecola were terrified to ride that bus with white folks.

After my father died and we moved to Barberton, I also began to realize the significance of an incident involving Aunt Emma and me. On that day, Miss Pecola didn't attend the Red Sox game with us. While we were coming home from the game, I informed Aunt Emma I was thirsty and I wanted some water. Aunt Emma didn't say anything, but we just kept walking. Finally, I started crying, screaming, "I want some water."

She entered a diner style restaurant and I believed I was about to receive some water. However, I didn't get any water, and I began to cry louder. "Don't worry, I'm going to get you some water," Aunt Emma insisted.

We went into two or three other restaurants and still I got no water. Finally, we went into a bar, and again my Aunt Emma was talking to someone. Again, she turned and walked away with no water. Then a white lady behind the counter motioned for me to come behind the bar and she handed me a cup of water. I remember thanking the lady because my Momma had always taught me to be polite, and Aunt Emma thanked her over and over.

It was a few years later that I realized that the episode was my first exposure to racism. Then I realized that we were being denied water because those were white restaurants. Given how my aunt reacted at the bus stop, it probably took courage for her to even enter a white restaurant.

In the 1960s, racial tension was an issue all over America, but I was comfortable growing up in Barberton. Certainly when you live in a city where the black population resides in one section of the town and whites live everywhere else, you realize there are racial barriers that cannot be ignored. There were older black people in Snydertown that warned me "to be careful of the white folks."

However, I was treated well by classmates and teammates in Barberton. I only had one scary racial moment when growing up in a town of 35,000, and I helped put myself in danger by allowing my temper to rule over my intelligence.

While a student at U.L. Light Middle School, I was strolling down the main street of Barberton one day when a car-full of older white boys drove by me in what I recall to be a 1957 Chevy Convertible.

"Hey you black m—f—," someone yelled.

"Get out of here n—r."

Rage filled me, and I yelled something about their mothers. There were four or five of them in the car, and they were a few years older than I was. However, I kept yelling until the car screeched to a halt. Those in the backseat vaulted out of the car, and I took off running down the street as if my life depended upon it, and maybe it did.

In full sprint, I turned into the alley adjacent to Sam Sing's laundry. There was a big dumpster and trashcans there and I ducked behind them. I was kneeling down with my eyes bugging, my body shaking and truly regretting what I had said to get myself into this predicament. I could hear them running past my hiding place. I stayed hidden 10 or 15 minutes, making sure my would-be assailants were long gone. Even then, I wasn't comfortable, and I bolted to the back door of Sing's Laundry. Mr. Sing answered the door. He was shocked to see the fear in my eyes. "Little Taylor, what's wrong?"

"Momma," I said. "I need Momma."

Momma didn't have a racist bone in her body, and she had taught us to respect people of all colors. That's why a conversation I had with her one night after one of my football games surprised me.

That evening I had scored a couple of touchdowns to help the Barberton Magics win a big game. The cheerleaders told me they were coming by my house to take me out for pizza to celebrate.

These cheerleaders, all white and as cute as they could be, drove up in front of my house and blew their horn repeatedly. My mother, sitting on the couch, just reached over and pushed down one of the sections of the venetian blinds to peep outside. "Lord have mercy, Jesus," she said. "What's going on with all of these white girls outside my house?"

I started laughing. "Those are just cheerleaders taking me out for a celebration," I answered. "They are just taking you?" she asked. When I said it was going to be just the cheerleaders and me, she seemed alarmed. "Boy," she said, "you had better be careful with all of those white girls."

I could see she was concerned, and that bothered me. When I came home, it was well past midnight. I wasn't surprised to see the blinds crack open as I was walking up to the house. I knew she would be sitting up, worrying about me.

"You all right?" she asked. "I'm fine," I said.

Right then I decided to extract my mother's feelings about the race issue. I asked her why she was so concerned about my decision to hang out with the white cheerleaders.

"Son, I don't want you to get hurt," she said. "A lot of white people don't like black boys hanging out with white girls." I insisted I would be okay, because I knew those girls from school. We were just classmates. "I don't think the girls would hurt you, but their parents might," she said.

My mother had grown up at a time when black men were still getting lynched in the deep south. She told me that even in the black community of Mound Bayou, Mississippi, she recalled there was a young white teen-age girl who was hanging out with a black teen-age boy. Her parents had discovered the relationship. "And the black boy disappeared," Momma told me.

Finally, at the end of the conversation, I asked her the most difficult question I probably ever asked her. Remember she was a kind, gentle woman who didn't want to speak ill of any of God's children. "What would you say if I were to marry a white woman," I asked.

Her newspaper toppled over, and she peered over the top of her glasses: "Oh child, I wouldn't want you to do that."

"What if I loved her?" I asked.

"Son, that would be fine, but it's not that simple," she said. "There would be problems. Marriage itself is not easy, but when you marry outside of your race, somebody will cause you problems. Her daddy, or brother—someone is not going to like you."

It was an honest answer from a woman who cared deeply about her son's happiness. Essentially when I left Barberton, I understood racism, but I probably did not view it as the impediment to success that it really was. Going to Ann Arbor also probably gave me a false sense of security about the issue, because the campus is located in a liberal community. Students on Michigan's campus in those years embraced every liberal cause known to man, including racial equality. And Bo truly was colorblind when it came to his players. He yelled at all players, regardless of their color. In my four years at Michigan, I never saw one instance of a black player treated differently because of his race. That just wouldn't happen with Bo in command.

The times were certainly influencing my thoughts about racial injustice. Remember Dr. Martin Luther King was assassinated in April of my freshman year at Michigan. The Black Action Movement was starting to gain a foothold on campuses around the country. Bo didn't want us to become involved in the protests, or even politics of the times. However, it was difficult not to become involved. Dr. King had made us all understand the need for black pride.

My feelings about racism have also always reflected the idea that I felt I should be racial, but not racist. I certainly understand that even today there is an uneven playing field for African Americans, particularly in education, for example.

When I graduated from college in 1971, I probably had a heightened sense of racial injustice. My perspective was keenly changed by the trip I made to Vietnam between my junior and senior season. I was a member of a goodwill USO group sent to talk to the troops. Rick Jason, who starred as Lieutenant Hanley in the TV series *Combat!*, was a member of my group, along with Herb Orvis of Colorado who ended up playing with the Detroit Lions, my Michigan teammate Glenn Doughty, New Mexico player Gary Cousins and New Mexico's coach Rudy Feldman. We were coming in as Bob Hope was leaving.

We visited firebases throughout Vietnam from December 17, 1970 to January 7, 1971. I was shocked by what I saw and heard. Flying into Saigon you could see massive craters everywhere, and I remember pondering how much explosives were required to create such destruction. Our involvement in the war was winding down when I was there, and most of the soldiers were numb about the horrors they had seen. They talked as if they no longer valued human life, particularly the lives of the Vietnamese. I hate to say that, but it's the truth. When I talked to the black soldiers in the country, many said they felt as if they had been discriminated against by their own army. Soldiers told me about the Long Binh Jail, or "LBJ" as they called it, where U.S. soldiers were imprisoned for crimes. It seemed inconceivable to me that a soldier could be serving his country and end up imprisoned by fellow troops. Both white and black troops told me the LBJ was a hellhole, although we weren't allowed to visit it. How could a black soldier be fighting for his country, and race issues still be in play? When I was there, it was clear to me that there were an inordinate number of African Americans and minorities fighting in this war. According to what soldiers told me, there were a disproportionate number of black men in LBJ.

It appalled me to see the debilitating wounds that were suffered by our soldiers. When we visited one hospital ship, I met one soldier whose head was swollen as a large as a basketball. He was only 21 or 22. Shrapnel wounds covered his entire body. One arm and one leg had been blown off. But his most hideous damage was to his abdomen. It was still open. He lifted up his bandage, and I could see into his rib cage. His organs were visible. They couldn't even close him up for some reason. It was difficult for me to look at him. However, he had remembered me from the 1969 Ohio State-Michigan game. He wanted to talk football. I'm thinking, *How could this man be talking football when his insides are hanging out?*

The man's courage both overwhelmed me and saddened me at the same time.

Our group was in Danang and the Vietnamese were celebrating TET. We were sprawled on our bunks, with the big Casablanca fans above us. It was ridiculously hot. I remember people were firing live ammo to celebrate. Glenn and I were hiding under our bunks, believing some of those bullets going into the air would eventually land. We should have known this was not going to be the Club Med when they gave us vaccinations against the bubonic plague, diphtheria and malaria before we entered the Southeast Asian country. I remember Bo telling Glenn and me that we needed to think about whether we truly wanted to go, because we had to sign a waiver that stipulated that if we were killed in Vietnam our families couldn't sue the U.S. Army.

Technically, we were in combat zones, but there were no close calls. One night we were lying in our bunks in boxer shorts and t-shirts. Our boots were off, and that was really against the rules. We had been advised to always keep our boots on our feet. We understood why that was a rule when there was a large boom that shook us out of our cots.

"They are bombing. They are bombing," someone was yelling. Doughty and I raced for the safety of a bunker like we were trying to hit the hole against Ohio State. Bo would have been proud of our quickness. The problem: the camp was on ground cinders, which are jagged rocks. We tore up our feet getting into that bunker. I can't tell you how close the bombing came to our location, but it definitely shook the camp.

By the time I left Vietnam, I was disappointed about the lack of progress that had been made in the area of civil rights. I felt as if black soldiers were being victimized in their military service. It seemed as if the U.S. government was being hypocritical by trying to defend the Vietnamese people while allowing unfair treatment of black soldiers.

By 1971, I was probably in my most militant period of thinking. When you factor in that I was severely depressed over the death of my mother, it's not surprising that any event that smacked of injustice was going to trigger a quick emotional response from me.

That's what happened at the Coaches All-American game in Lubbock, Texas, in the summer of 1971. Not even Bo Schembechler could calm me down. In fact, he was an innocent victim of my anger.

Bo's approach to football was basic. He was a very complicated man. He ruled through intimidation. Honestly, I thought underneath his rough husk there was a soft core. I believed he cared for me deeply, and I thought I could call him and talk about any personal problem I might have. Maybe our relationship was a bit unique because we were both from Barberton, Ohio, but I believe that if you quiz most Michigan men about their relationship with Bo they would probably offer that he looked out for their well being at one time or another. If you were experiencing grade struggles, or even family or personal problems, Bo often knew about them before you did.

Obviously, Bo was aware that my father had died when I was very young, and maybe he tried to be a father figure to me. When my mother died, I was despondent to the point that I didn't want to return to Michigan to finish my degree that semester. I had no desire to try pro football. But it was Bo and the Mellow Men who reminded me, "Bill, you got to get back up!" It was Bo's words that slapped me back to reality. "Your mother would want you to finish your degree," he said.

Once I returned to Ann Arbor, Bo had me thinking again about football and my future. My mother's death had prevented me from playing in the All-American Game in Florida, and Bo wanted me to play in the Coaches All-American All-Star Game in Lubbock, Texas on June 24, 1972. At the time, this game was considered the kickoff game for the next season. Legendary Alabama coach Paul "Bear" Bryant would be the head coach of the East Squad and Bo was going to be one of his assistants. He was going to be working with the backfield, which meant he would be working with me.

On February 1, 1972, the Atlanta Falcons had selected me in the fifth round—109th overall—in the NFL draft. I realized that practicing and playing down in the stifling Texas heat would certainly help get me ready for the Falcons' training camp. Through Bo's help, I had begun to regain my focus. I began to understand that my mother would have wanted me to pursue my dream. There was another reason to go—my buddies, Thom Darden, Reggie McKenzie and Mike Taylor were also going.

Football under the Texas sun in late June can be torturous, but the week in Lubbock started out as great fun. O.J. Simpson was there working as an analyst for the televised broadcast. I had met him six months before at the Rose Bowl game in Pasadena and we had clicked. Remember he was only 24 at the time, and he was just a year or two older than the players in the game. Quickly Simpson—or "Juice" as we called him—formed up a posse and we all rode together a couple of evenings. By then, Simpson was already famous—he had captured a Heisman Trophy and was honored as the NFL Rookie of the Year while playing for the Buffalo Bills. He was still a few months away from winning his first NFL rushing title, and he didn't become the first player in NFL history to rush for 2,000 yards in a season until 1973. Maybe a year or two later, we would have been even more in awe of him, but down in Lubbock Simpson seemed like one of the guys.

The night before the game, he took a bunch of us to one of his friend's home and we had a great meal of red beans and rice. Funny what you remember. It was so good. We ate and ate until we couldn't move.

Over the next two years, I got to know Simpson even better because my buddy Reggie McKenzie, one of the Mellow Men, became his lead blocker in Buffalo. "BT, I see how you gained all of those yards at Michigan running behind McKenzie," Simpson said to me once.

Not that Simpson and I were best friends, but I broke enough bread with the man to understand who he was and what he was about. When he was accused of murdering his ex-wife, I told friends that the man I knew was not a murderer. I believed that back then, and I still believe that today.

After the first couple of practices on the Texas Tech campus in Lubbock, it was clear that I was the No. 1 tailback. I was running strong and protecting the football. Midweek I had to leave practice to travel to Washington D.C. where I was being honored for being one of *Sport Magazine's* Players of the Month during my senior season. The honor was a luncheon with President Richard Nixon and his wife Pat. We were able to shake his hand.

Famed Washington power broker Vernon Jordan, extremely active in the civil rights movement, showed us around Washington. My family was primarily Democratic. We were strong supporters of President John F. Kennedy for his civil rights work and to Lyndon Johnson for following through on JFK's civil rights agenda. Somehow, the family—myself included—had a unique affinity for President Nixon. When you are a poor black family, your No. 1 political issue is employment and being able to put food on the table. During Nixon's tenure in office, all of my brothers and sisters had found good jobs and we credited him with bringing some unprecedented prosperity to our corner of the world in Barberton. My brother Thomas was even working simultaneously in two different automobile plants. My mother had taught me to respect America's leaders. I remember when I was very young, my mother had been fascinated by President Eisenhower. "There's old Ike on the TV," she would say, and we would all have to stop and watch. I had heard that President Nixon was a college football fan, and I had even sent a letter to President Nixon inviting him to attend a Michigan game during my senior year.

I couldn't persuade myself to ask President Nixon for an autograph, but I asked Jordan if he would ask the President to sign a picture. A few weeks later, a picture arrived in the mail, personalized to me and signed by the President.

This could have ended up one of the most interesting weeks of my life, but the trials and tribulations that have defined my life were only just beginning.

Ironically, it was O.J. Simpson who notified me that there was an emergency back home in Ohio. He was in the lobby of the dormitory to pick me up, and he called upstairs to tell me that my cousin had just called the front desk from Akron. He said I needed to call home immediately.

The horror of the news that I received overwhelmed me with grief. Grief devoured me. My Uncle Eugene Wells, the man who had consoled me six months before when my mother had died suddenly, had used his gun to shoot and kill my Aunt Hattie in their home on Orlando Street in Akron. He then turned the gun on himself and committed suicide. Many of his children were present in the house when the killings occurred upstairs. Even today, it remains a true mystery of why my uncle, a man who had worked extremely hard to have a decent life, would suddenly decide to bring this level of tragedy down upon his family.

My family and friends said my uncle would have wanted me to play. They convinced me to stay and play the game before coming home for the funeral. Who knows whether it was the right decision, because when I look back now I realize that my mind was in a dangerous place. I returned to the practice field, but was I really there? I wasn't thinking clearly. Now I realize that anger and despondency were building up in me and that I had started to look for anyway I could find to cope. It wouldn't be too many months later that alcohol and drugs would become my refuge from the pain in my heart and my mind. There were signs in Lubbock that my life was coming unhinged, and that I was slipping down the road to depression. At that point, maybe anger was more prevalent than alcohol as my escape from the pain.

On the night of the game, my anger boiled over. I became involved in a misunderstanding with Bo Schembechler that left us not speaking for perhaps a year.

During practice all week, I had been the tailback with the first-team offense ahead of Alabama All-American Johnny Musso. In my mind, I deserved to be No. 1. He had rushed for 1,088 yards in 1971 and I had gained 1,297 yards that season. But it wasn't about statistics. I just believed I was a more dynamic offensive player.

Before leaving for Washington DC to be honored at the White House, I believed I had established myself as the starting tailback. When I returned, Musso was first string. But in the final two practice sessions, it was clear to me that I had regained the No. 1 job. I and everyone else understood that, or so I thought.

During pre-game warm-ups, Bo came up to me and said, "We are going to start Johnny Musso."

As I was walking away I said, "That's bullshit."

Somehow, Bo misheard what I was saying. "Are you calling me a racist?" he screamed as he grabbed me by the shoulder.

"That was bullshit," I repeated. "I should start."

Bo pushed me, and I pushed him back. I remember looking up into the stands and seeing Bo's wife, Millie, right above us. She had the most puzzled look on her face. She just couldn't believe what she was witnessing on the sideline.

It was 107 degrees in Lubbock, and we were told that the temperature on the Tartan turf was 117 or higher. However, I was hotter than the field conditions. Although I never said Bo was racist, I felt as if there was racism hidden in Bryant's decision. It smelled of racial politics. Musso was white and I was black. We weren't in the Midwest. We were in Texas where the redneck attitude was still prevalent in 1972. We weren't that far removed from the civil rights struggles of the 1960s.

Ron Johnson had become the first black captain at Michigan in 1968, and he had endured racism in that season. Michigan Coach Bump Elliott was concerned enough about Johnson's safety during a road game at Duke that he actually considered not playing him. Johnson did elect to play. He was my fraternity brother, and he told me later that each time he left the field the white fans in the stands taunted him with racial slurs. It was a scary situation in Durham, North Carolina.

A year later, I essentially succeeded Johnson as Michigan's featured back. It did not seem like a stretch for me to conclude that strains of racism were still present in the summer of 1972 in Lubbock, Texas.

At the time, maybe I was mad at Bo for not standing up to Bryant when he wanted to start Musso who played for him at Alabama. After the confrontation, I walked as far away from Bo and Bear as I could. I sat by myself on the bench. Even those who didn't see Bo and me arguing knew there was a problem.

The heated pre-game discussion didn't alter my status. Musso started the first series of the game. But on our second offensive series, Bo put me in the game. I was so fueled by anger that I could have run through a wall of fire. Michigan State's Ron Curl had blocked a punt, and I dove in for the score on the next play to make it a 7-0 game.

By the end of the game, I had rushed for more than 90 yards and 17 carries and scored two touchdowns. I also had a couple of 20-yard runs in the third quarter to set up touchdowns. By the end of the game, my East squad had defeated the West 42-20 and I was named the game's Most Valuable Player. A $1,000 scholarship was sent to Michigan in my name. I played with vengeance. I played with anger. I had made my point.

In the heat of the moment, I blamed Bo for the situation and I should not have done that. Honestly, I never said or even implied, that Bo was a racist. That was a misunderstanding because I knew Bo well enough to know that he did not make decisions based on the color of a player's skin. However, in my heart, I believed that Bear Bryant had made a racist decision. It came across to me as discrimination. He had a white southern running back and he had a black northern running back. The black running back was better. He chose to start the white running back. I knew I was the best running back on the East squad, and I proved that in that game by performing as well as I did.

Bo and I were on the same plane going back to Michigan, and we didn't speak. Millie Schembechler was upset. I could see the sadness in Bo over the incident. I could tell he was hurt. Maybe I was too mad. Maybe I was too immature at the time but I didn't try to resolve the issue immediately even though it tore me up inside. It's impossible for me to describe the mix of rage, grief and isolation I felt on that long plane trip home after the Coaches All-American Bowl.

When I saw the caskets with my Uncle and Aunt lying in them, it was as if my last few layers of normalcy had crumbled around me. I didn't know it at the time but it was going to be a quarter of a century before my mind was restored to health. And I also didn't know at the time that the grief and tragedy was just beginning in my life.

Bo and I didn't speak for at least a year. People in the Michigan family were aware that Bo and I had issues that needed to be resolved. I remember talking to former Michigan player Tom Goss about the episode, along with other "M" men like Mike Oldham, Mike Taylor and Reggie McKenzie. They called and urged me to make my peace with Bo.

Finally, I swallowed my pride, went into his office, and cleared the air about the miscommunication that occurred on the sideline in Lubbock. I can't remember what was said, or even whether I apologized. I do recall that I made sure that he understood that I never said, or believed, he was a racist. The entire conversation only lasted 15 minutes. When we were finished, Bo and I had our relationship restored.

When I look back today, I can see that my life had already begun to unravel by the time I had arrived in Lubbock. My steep descent into a hellish existence, maybe triggered by my mother's death, was well underway. My religious faith, a foundation in my life since childhood, had begun to wane. When my uncle and aunt died under tragic circumstances, I became angrier with God.

Today I can see that my confrontation with Bo on the sidelines was just a symptom of the depression and rage that I was enduring. It hurts me to think of how my relationship with Bo was temporarily fractured because he would prove again three years later that I have no better friend and ally than Bo Schembechler. When society was branding me a criminal, Bo supported me and did all that he could to assist me. Bo was a powerful man, but not even he could prevent me from taking the deep fall I took on January 17, 1975.

CHAPTER 7

ATLANTA IS NOT ANN ARBOR

W<small>HAT</small> I <small>DIDN'T REALIZE WHEN</small> I <small>REPORTED</small> to the Atlanta Falcons' training camp in 1972, was that my emotional state was like a newly active volcano. To any observer, I was a mountain of tranquility. However, deep below the surface, pressure and rage were building at an alarming rate. The death of my mother, aunt and uncle and Valerie had turned me molten. The dangerous aspect of any volcano is that sometimes there are no signs that it is going to burst until lava and ashes are spewing over the landscape. My eruption was coming. I just didn't know it.

As an athlete, I was trained to hyper-focus on the next game or objective, and maybe that prevented me from recognizing the signs of my depression. Or maybe I simply didn't know what I didn't know. Today, I'm an educator, trained to recognize how the thought process works. Back in 1972, I didn't realize the turmoil that was churning through my mind and soul. I believed the only issue in my life was becoming a starting running back for the Falcons. I felt confident, or at least I acted that way. When I signed with the Falcons, I only wanted a one-year contract because I believed that I was going to establish myself as a National Football League star. I signed for $50,000, including a $10,000 signing bonus. My thinking was that I didn't want to be locked into a rookie-grade multi-year deal when I ran for 1,000 yards in my rookie season. Even as a rookie, I believed I would enjoy the same success I had in college. I understood that the NFL was a bigger challenge, but I had faith in my ability. Defenders were bigger, stronger and faster, but blockers were also bigger, stronger and faster. Coach Bo Schembechler had schooled me well in the art in climbing into the hip pocket of a blocker and following him into the end zone. To be a 1,000-yard rusher in the NFL, you needed to average about 71 yards per game over 14 games. Surely, a tailback who averaged more than 100 yards per game in college should be able to find his niche in the NFL. There was logic in that line of reasoning. After all, I had been a three-time All-American tailback for one of the most prestigious football programs in the country. Without question, I was considered one of the best college players in the nation. The college teams were the feeder system for the NFL. Isn't it logical to conclude that over the next few seasons one of the best college players of the 1971 season was going to become one of the best NFL players? The idea of failure didn't enter into my thinking, although there were signs that failure was possible.

The word in the scouting community was that I could be drafted as high as the second round, possibly going to the Kansas City Chiefs. The Chiefs' franchise featured running back and former Iowa standout, Ed Podolak who had gained almost 1,000 yards combined rushing and pass receiving. However, he was more of a utility player and they were looking at adding a workhorse back to reduce the wear and tear on Podolak with the hope of making him even more effective than he was. The Chiefs had won a Super Bowl in 1970 and the thought of playing for Coach Hank Stram was quite appealing. Even though I didn't know Stram, I had a sense that he was like Schembechler.

Nevertheless, on draft day the Chiefs elected to choose Nebraska running back Jeff Kinney with the 23rd pick in the first round. The Dallas Cowboys were supposedly looking for a running back in the second round, but they opted for Robert Newhouse out of Houston.

The second round ended and I was still there. The third round ended and I was still there. The fourth round ended and I was still there. Adding insult to my injured pride, Michigan State's Eric Allen—the player that Bo used to kid me about in practice—was the last pick in the fourth round. Johnny Musso, the back I thought I outperformed at the Coaches All-American game, was selected ahead of me.

Finally, with the fifth pick of the fifth round—109th overall—the Falcons selected me. I was the 16th running back chosen in the 1972 draft. I was the 5th member of the Mellow Men to be drafted. Darden had been selected 18th overall to Cleveland, followed by Mike Taylor 20th to the New York Jets. Reggie McKenzie went as the first pick in the second round to the Buffalo Bills. Glenn Doughty was selected 47th by the Baltimore Colts as a wide receiver. I was the 5th player from our house to be selected.

Although I was disappointed at how low I was taken in the draft, I wasn't crushed. When I reviewed the Falcons' roster, I realized that Cannonball Butler had been their leading ground gainer in 1971 and he hadn't even managed 600 yards on the ground.

I had broken Ron Johnson's Michigan rushing records at Michigan, and by the time I was drafted, Johnson had already recorded his first 1,000-yard season in the NFL. I had great respect for Johnson's ability. My feeling was that if Ron could gain 1,000 yards, I could as well.

To this day I can't say with any certainty why I slid in the draft, but the leading theory would be that teams were worried that my injury during my junior season had slowed me a step. Even playing with torn cartilage for five games that season, I still managed to gain more than 1,000 yards.

As I headed to the campus of Furman University in Greenville, South Carolina for the Falcons' training camp, I was determined to prove that the scouts had underestimated my ability. I could not have guessed that my NFL career would be over before it even started.

The first shock was just being in the south. Certainly growing up in the 1960s, I understood that in some places you are judged by the color of your skin instead of the value of your character. But I had not been made to feel uncomfortable in Barberton, and Ann Arbor was a very liberal community. The campus of Furman in 1972 was not like the campus of the University of Michigan in 1972. As a black man, I could feel the difference.

The other difference was that Van Brocklin was not Schembechler when it came to team diversity. Van Brocklin seemed to have respect for some of the black veterans, like Cannonball Butler for instance. However, if you were black and you were not an established premium player, he gave off the impression that you were just another black dude.

I also didn't like the way he conducted practices—going around to lineman in their stances and knocking them over.

Bo always had tough words for his players, but he treated everyone like that. That was his style. Players all liked and respected Bo. If Bo wasn't in your face, that's when you had to worry. I didn't get that same impression with Van Brocklin. He treated players differently, and it bothered me.

Once training camp started, my most aggravating irritation was not Van Brocklin. It was a jock rash that developed on the first day. My inner thighs were inflamed and were the color of raw hamburger. It wasn't uncommon at the start of training camp to develop a mild case of jock rash. Body folds (flexures) are prone to inflammatory rashes because of increased moisture. These areas are slightly warmer than other body areas, and friction from movement of adjacent skin results in chaffing. This increases susceptibility to infection by bacteria and yeasts. In the sweltering heat, you expected your inner thighs to become sensitive or raw. However, the case of jock rash I developed at Furman was the most severe I've ever seen. I wondered if they were washing the clothes with a detergent that was causing an allergic reaction. Initially, doctors were giving me a salve that I would lather onto the infected area. I would wrap it up in gauze and ace bandages, and then pull the pads over it. It was getting worse by the day. I have a vivid memory of lying on a table with my legs spread with a fan blowing on me to dry out the area and to provide some measure of relief. Not only was the area raw, but the sores were starting to break open. My condition became so severe that the doctor ordered that I be kept out of practice for four or five days so the area would heal. That clearly set me back.

When I returned to practice, I began to be bothered even more about Van Brocklin's treatment of black players. I'm not suggesting that he was disrespectful to every black player on the team. Van Brocklin had time for the black players he knew he needed. However, an average black player or an unproven rookie black player seemed to be subjected to degradation that I don't believe I would have experienced had I been drafted by a Northern-based team. I know the other Mellow Men, particularly Reggie McKenzie in Buffalo and Thom Darden in Cleveland, felt far more comfortable in their first training camps than I felt in mine.

Presumably, the Falcons' management and coaches were aware how I felt about the way black players were treated. I had discussions with other black players about the situation and there are no secrets on a football team.

I had been moved to fullback and I started the team's first exhibition game on the road against the San Diego Chargers on August 6, 1972. I had four carries and didn't gain a yard in a 30-7 loss. After the game, I was told to turn in my playbook. My NFL audition had lasted four carries. Van Brocklin never talked to me. In fact, no coach talked to me about the situation. I was just told that I was put on waivers. I was swept out the door with no explanation.

Although I was shocked by the decision, I wasn't initially angry because I had decided in my mind that I really didn't want to be in an organization where subtle racism seemed to still be present. At first, I was almost happy to leave.

However, within a couple of months, the anger about the experience had risen to the surface. When you consider the tragedy I had endured over seven months, it is surprising that it didn't come sooner.

When I was playing for the Calgary Stampeders in the Canadian Football League a couple of months later, I let my feelings become public in an article with *Akron-Beacon Journal* staff writer Rich Zitrin. I essentially told him that Van Brocklin managed his team like he was a plantation owner. Zitrin quoted me accurately in his article.

"He's a racist," I told him. "Speaking for my race, Van Brocklin is setting us back 100 years."

It was a strong statement, but I still stand by it today. That wasn't all that I said. My quotes were so strong that Zitrin simply let me vent for six consecutive paragraphs at one point in his story.

"I ran into a shaky situation," I told Zitrin. "It was a political thing. Competition there is based more on character and personality than on ability. With Van Brocklin, you're the slave. He's the master."

I told Zitrin that I had talked to veteran black players on the Falcons and they had similar complaints about Van Brocklin's coaching style.

"Everything is 'yes sir' and 'no sir.' The racial tones are obvious," I continued in the article. "It's hard to believe people stand for it."

In the story, I revealed that the black Atlanta players were frustrated and most of them would have left if they could. Remember, there was no measure of free agency when I came to the NFL in 1972.

"The black players would like to leave, but they stay around to pick up the paycheck. To me the money isn't worth it," I said in the article. "They could take the contract and shove it."

I explained about the degradation that I experienced during the public practice sessions. I did not tell Zitrin that Van Brocklin used the term "boy" when talking to black players.

"It was disrespect," I told Zitrin. "We'd have 200-300 people watching our practices and Van Brocklin would cuss us out and belittle us in front of everyone. The next second he'd come over and pat you and his mood had changed. He expected you to smile at him…I didn't blow anything down there. But I had to decide whether I wanted to be a man and respect myself or become someone I didn't want to be."

The most interesting aspect of that story is that Zitrin, in the interest of writing both sides of the story, called the Falcons' office to get Van Brocklin's reaction to my accusations. The Falcons' Public Reaction Director Wilt Browning told Zitrin that he didn't think Van Brocklin would want to "get involved in this."

Someone was calling Van Brocklin a "racist," and he wouldn't want to get involved? To me, when someone doesn't defend his own honor, he is in essence, making a statement.

The other element of Zitrin's story that seems to add more credibility to my claim is Browning's quotes about the situation:

First, Browning said I had been cut because "we found Taylor was unable to turn the corner. We needed someone to get outside."

He claimed that's why the team traded for Dave Hampton who is also black. Then Browning added, "Taylor has speed, but it's a strange speed. It's mostly from tackle to tackle."

Correct me if I'm wrong, but don't most NFL coaches covet running backs who can run between the tackles with quickness to the hole?

Browning's most damning quote came when he tried to defend the Falcons' record in race relations.

"We drafted Clarence Ellis (out of Notre Dame) No. 1, not because he's colored, but because he's a very fine ball player," Browning told Zitrin in the article that was published on October 26, 1972 that "Taylor is disgruntled because he was a very fine college player and hasn't been able to make it in the pros."

Browning's use of the term "colored" would seem to be telling. I wasn't trying to make this southern-based team in the 1950s or 1960s. This was 1972, eight years after the landmark Civil Rights legislation, seven years after the march on Selma, four years after Doctor Martin Luther King was assassinated. Correct me if I'm wrong, but didn't Dr.

King essentially give his life to the hope that black men and women would not be subjected to degradation because of the color of their skin? When Browning used the derogatory term "colored" in the interview with Zitrin, soon-to-be President Jimmy Carter was already Governor of Georgia. He had championed black voting rights and when he became Governor in 1970 he had declared that the "era of segregation" was over.

The fact that Browning would still publicly use a derogatory description for a black man at this time supports my contention that the Falcons' organization was slow to change with the times.

In explaining why I was cut, Falcons' personnel director Tom Braatz told the *Akron Beacon Journal*: "Billy hadn't played well since he had been in camp. He just wasn't as good as the running backs in camp."

Atlanta's backs when I was cut were Butler, Art Malone, Harmon Wages, Joe Profit and Paul Gipson. Butler never played another down for Atlanta and was out of football a year later. Wages wasn't able to play in 1972 because of injury and rushed for 47 yards in 1973. Gipson never played for the Falcons. Profit gained 132 yards for the Falcons in 1972 and was gone by the end of the following season. Malone had a very good season in 1972—rushing for 798 yards and catching 50 passes. He turned out to be a very dependable NFL back. My point is that given the Falcons' running back uncertainty at the time, there was plenty of reason to give the Big Ten Most Valuable Player of 1971 a significant opportunity to make a NFL roster in 1972. Four carries do not represent a significant opportunity.

My presumption is that coaches were looking for reasons to get rid of me because they perceived me as a troublemaker because I had talked to my teammates about Van Brocklin's treatment of black players.

Van Brocklin died in 1983 and I considered not discussing this situation out of respect for the fact that he is not present to defend what happened in 1972. Yet he was aware of what I said in 1972 and chose not to respond to the *Akron Beacon Journal*. To be honest, when I reflect back on that time, my feelings haven't changed. However, I want to be fair here: this is a short segment of Van Brocklin's time on earth. I know he was a great quarterback who was inducted into the Hall of Fame the year before I met him. For all I know, the man lived an exemplary life beyond the days of that training camp. However, I do know that the way he treated black men at the 1972 Atlanta Falcons' training camp was offensive to me.

Three decades after that event, I can see more clearly what happened to my professional career. While I stand by my comments about Van Brocklin during that period, the truth is that I wasn't ready to play professional football when I showed up at the Falcons' training camp. Could I have survived and played through my problems had I been at another training camp? Probably, if I had been with Reggie McKenzie in Buffalo or maybe with Thom Darden at Cleveland. I believe I could have pulled it together to have some form of a career. If one of the Mellow Men had been by my side in the Atlanta training camp, maybe I would have persevered. However, I can't be sure of that. Anger was festering deep within me. The deaths of my mother, Aunt Hattie, Uncle Eugene and Valerie had numbed me at first. But it was like the anesthesia had worn off and now I was feeling torturous pain. By that time, I was already in the early stages of alcohol abuse. I was drinking too much, although at the time I had no idea how alcoholism was starting to rule my life.

Almost as soon as the Falcons cut me, the St. Louis Cardinals claimed me on waivers. In the first few practices, I was running in the backfield with Donnie Anderson. The Cardinals assigned Ahmad Rashad to be my roommate, and that was a treat. At the time his name was Bobby Moore, and he was drafted fourth overall out of Oregon State. He was the first offensive player chosen in the draft. He owned this cherry red Cadillac convertible with a white top and I remember having a good time hanging out with Rashad.

Bob Holloway was the coach there and he treated me well, but the rash wouldn't go away completely and I was nursing a couple of injuries, the most troublesome of which was the left knee. It was clear that the damage I suffered as a junior was having a prolonged impact. The Cardinals' team physician put me on a machine to test my leg strength and the left knee was only working at 60-70 percent capacity of where it needed to be. It's difficult to make a roster of a NFL team when you are facing that level of deficiency. The Cardinals eventually let me go, and I had no ill will toward that organization. In the short time I was there, they made me part of the team.

From there I ended up with the Stampeders where I actually did play during the regular season. I had some adjustment issues. In Canada, teams get three downs, instead of four. Also, the field is 10 yards longer and almost 12 yards wider. The end zone is 20 yards long, instead of 10. If your team is on the opponent's 20-yard line, the quarterback could still call a post pattern. Each team uses 12 players, instead of 11. Really, it's a different dynamic. It's a passing game and more wide open.

I did return to Calgary for the 1973 season, but I was injured again and ended up getting waived. Although I was disenchanted with the NFL after my experience in Atlanta, I decided to give it another shot and accepted a training camp tryout with the Philadelphia Eagles. Roman Gabriel was the quarterback. I had watched him when I was kid. Now he was 33 and I was in the huddle with him. I was really on cloud nine. In the preseason when he handed me the ball I wanted to shake his hand.

Although I was cut before the regular season, it was a good experience for me. I came to Philadelphia before training camp to work out. I lived with former Michigan cornerback Randy Logan. We had fun together. He wore an African-style tam. To tease him, I would call him "Imaranda Loganda."

The Eagles' No. 1 receiver was Harold Carmichael, a 6'-8" athlete with sweet hands. Today, he's considered the greatest receiver in Eagles' history. Back then, I had never seen a receiver that tall. I had some fun with Harold. I called him Sky Man.

When he would bend over in the huddle, his big shadow would suddenly cover everyone. He was like a human eclipse.

"Damn, Sky Man, what's it like up there?" I would say to Harold. "What are you talking about Taylor?" he asked. "I mean what's the atmosphere like up there?" I said. "Can you breathe? I know the air has to be thinner up there." Everyone in the huddle doubled over in laughter.

Good times didn't translate into a lengthy stay in Philadelphia. I really felt my football career was over. I took some graduate classes and got a job working at General Motors in Flint, Michigan. The idea of playing again didn't enter my mind until the World Football League was formed. When the Memphis Southmen offered me a contract for $25,000, I accepted without much hesitation. I told the *Akron Beacon-Journal* reporter Zitrin in May of 1974 that I just couldn't shake football out of my system. I tried to push football out of my mind, but when I watched it on television and read about it during the fall of 1973, I felt as if I wasn't ready to give it up.

"I probably have a good future with GM and everything is okay, but I need to carry the ball," I told Zitrin.

I had come back to Akron to stay with my brother Jimmie while I trained. I was excited about playing in Memphis because I had lived there until I was five. I still had family living there.

In the article, Zitrin noted that I was originally trying to avoid beer while I was in training, and then changed the plan by adding five minutes of running into morning workout for every Budweiser I would drink. The fact that I had trouble staying away from booze even when I was training was probably an indication of where I was heading.

At 25, I knew I was looking at my last chance at a professional football career. The WFL seemed like a perfect fit for me because the rosters were filled with second-chance or last-chance players, or older players who were just trying to hang on to their careers.

"I feel good about the WFL," I told Zitrin. "It's new and it can't afford to bicker over how long your hair is or what color your eyes are or who your friends are. My back is against the wall. If I don't make it this time, people can say I was just one of the guys who couldn't cut it. I'm in the same boat as the league. We both have to prove we're here to stay. Now it's a matter of show and tell."

Obviously, Zitron was aware of the tragedies that had overwhelmed me since I left Michigan. I acknowledged that the deaths had made it difficult for me to concentrate on football.

"Now I have enough freedom of mind to deal with everything," I told him. "Now football can be No. 1 again. You can't be successful and have it any other way."

The last sentence I spoke was the truth, but the first two sentences were lies, although I probably didn't even realize that I wasn't being honest. Clearly, I was still in the midst of depression, aggravated by a growing dependence upon alcohol. The restlessness I felt was probably a symptom of my condition. I was still angry. I may have loved football, but it was difficult, maybe impossible, for me to concentrate on the sport the way I had under Schembechler's command in Ann Arbor.

The Southmen situation didn't work out for me, and I ended up with the WFL's Chicago Fire. The best moment on the field came in an away game against Southern California when the last defender brought me down on a kickoff return. It was only a 26-yard return, but I vividly remember seeing nothing but open field if I could have eluded that tackler.

Truthfully, the best moment playing for the Chicago Fire was when I lined up in the backfield next to former Cleveland Browns running back Leroy Kelly. He was one of my idols growing up in Barberton. I admired the way he bulled his way through the defensive line, with defenders hanging on him as he ran. He seemed like such a big, powerful back when I was young and I remember standing next to him and realizing he was just an inch taller than me and probably close to the same weight.

One time the ball was about to be snapped and I was thinking, "I'm in the same backfield with a player who played in the same backfield with Jim Brown." It was an awesome feeling.

There weren't many shining moments in 1974. By the time the Chicago Fire forfeited its final game of the season because the franchise was failing, I had already been waived.

The WFL continued in 1975 without me. Another failed attempt at professional football left me more disillusioned. It's impossible to accurately reflect how I was feeling in those days because depression clouded my thinking and my judgment. Since my grade school days, I had always been pointed toward an objective. My feet were always racing toward a goal line. But when my career was over in the WFL, I had no primary direction.

Now 31 years later, I have a clear understanding of why I wasn't able to live my professional dream. Even in my depressed state it was evident to me that I had more raw ability than some players who did make the cut. However, other factors brought me down before I ever reached the line of scrimmage.

First, I tried out for six teams over two years and was never fully healthy in any of my tryouts. Second, depression took me down better than any linebacker ever could. After my mother died, and three people close to me were killed violently, I didn't recognize that I needed counseling. I didn't recognize that I was suffering from a mental illness that was preventing me from fully exploring my potential. I also didn't see that I was trying to treat my mental wounds with daily doses of alcohol. When I should have been mentally preparing myself for my NFL opportunity, I was wallowing in self-pity. I believed I was going to die. When the NFL scouts were coming around campus with their stopwatches and tape measures after the season, they must have heard that I wasn't working out with my teammates. I was working out, and my performance in Lubbock proved that, but if I had been working out with my teammates, they might have pushed me harder.

Starting in Atlanta may have doomed me before I started. Based on my mental state, could there have been a worse environment for me at that time in my life? The treatment that I received there simply fed my rage. If I could have started elsewhere—in Detroit where I was well known or with my hometown team, the Cleveland Browns—it might have been different. I had proven in college that I had the will to play through injuries, but I was too angry to do that in Atlanta. If I had been in Detroit, Cleveland or any city where a black man was made to feel welcome, then maybe I would have been given a longer opportunity to prove myself.

Through the years I have realized that there was another important reason for my struggles that never would have occurred to me back in those days. I didn't have a father to mentor me through the rough spots. When I was young, I remember going off by myself and crying about my father. I had a vivid memory of seeing him in his coffin in the church, and asking my mom, "Why was Daddy sleeping in church?" I only knew my dad five years, and yet I missed him dearly. When I was in college, I still missed him, especially when I saw the other Mellow Men, relating to their fathers. I probably needed counseling, but back then, young black men didn't think in those terms.

When I reminisce about the Mellow Men, I have as much fondness for the parents as much as I do the players. I recall that Sam Carpenter was a tremendous influence on his son. Thom Darden leaned on his father heavily for support, as did Glenn Doughty. When I was at Michigan, I didn't miss not having a father because Schembechler was there to serve as my father figure. He was an inspirational figure.

I remember Sam Carpenter helping me through some difficult times in college. If I had issues, Butch would say, "What's your class schedule? Let's drive up to Flint and see my dad." Sometimes we would stay all weekend and I would feel better when I left.

The time between the death of my mother and the first training camp was only six months. It was only a few months after Valerie was killed and only weeks after my Aunt Hattie and Uncle Eugene were gone. At that point, I really did believe that I would be the next to die.

I was in so much pain that summer that I truly considered not playing professional football. I think I knew I was in trouble emotionally. However, there was no father there to guide me when the situation in Atlanta seemed intolerable. Maybe I should have called Sam Carpenter and told him how I was feeling. I didn't do that. Maybe if one of the Mellow Men would have been in Atlanta it would have been different. No matter where I was, I think would have survived if I had one of my close teammates with me. I felt alone. I just allowed myself to become angrier and angrier.

Today I also know that playing professional football is a long-shot proposition even for the best college athletes. All of the Mellow Men were drafted in the NFL draft in 1972, but only McKenzie, Doughty and Darden had lengthy careers. Darden played nine seasons with the Cleveland Browns, while Doughty played eight seasons for the Baltimore Colts. Reggie McKenzie had a lengthy career with Buffalo.

Frankly, these three players were super prepared for the next level—much more than I was prepared because of a variety of factors. Even though Mike Taylor was a first round pick, he only ended up playing a couple of seasons in the NFL. He was bothered by injuries as well, and then he tried to squeeze out a few extra dollars by jumping to the WFL with the Detroit Wheels. However, when that league folded, he didn't get back to the NFL. Mike Oldham was drafted in the 10th round by the Washington Redskins, but chose not to tryout.

When my gridiron career was officially over, I was not prepared for life after football. I should have been ready because I had a bachelor's degree from the University of Michigan. However, my thinking was way out of bounds. The angst and sorrow inside me was overwhelming me to the point of exhaustion. I was weary about thinking of what the future would hold. I drank to forget and in the morning, I would remember that I was jobless and broke. I was starting to move away from trusted friends and toward new acquaintances.

The pressure and anger inside had become a critical mass. Cracks were appearing in my confidence, and resentment was bubbling to the surface. I was nearing my breaking point. When my eruption finally came in 1975, it did as much damage to my life as the Vesuvius eruption did to Pompei in 79 AD. My eruption buried me, and it took many years for me to dig out.

CHAPTER 8

25 MINUTES OF REGRET

FEAR DOES NOT COME WHEN YOU ARE a Michigan tailback running off tackle against the Ohio State Buckeyes in Columbus. Fear comes when three police cars surround your vehicle and officers, with guns drawn, demand that you raise your hands in the air or they will "blow your head off."

I faced that situation on January 17, 1975, when I was arrested on a Barberton, Ohio, street in connection with a failed bank robbery.

As I stepped out of the car with my hands raised one of the police officers said, "Oh, my God, it's Billy Taylor."

The shame and embarrassment I felt at that moment cannot be described. As I lay spread-eagle across the hood of the car, it was as if I was walking through a nightmare wishing someone would wake me up. It was as if I was having an out-of-body experience, and I could see myself being handcuffed and pushed into the squad car. I remember thinking, *I'm glad my mother isn't alive to see this day.*

Three years to the day after the City of Barberton had hosted a "Billy Taylor Day" to honor my football accomplishments at the University of Michigan, I became involved in a criminal enterprise that left me branded as a convicted felon for the rest of my life.

When we arrived at the police station, news reporters and photographers were already there. I pulled my hands to my face and dipped my head to prevent a clear photo. That's the photo that was published all over the country the next morning. America loves the story of a small town boy becoming a sports hero, but an All-American football player becoming a criminal also sells newspapers. There was no Court TV in those days, but my humiliation seemed just as public. Everyone in Barberton knew that Billy Taylor had been arrested minutes after it happened.

The new chamber of hell I had entered was made clear to me when I was put in a holding cell with another prisoner. I didn't even know the guy's name, but I remember he was feeling a lot of pressure about being incarcerated. Everyone handles these situations differently, and I had my own conversation with myself going on in my head. I was already thinking, *how am I going to recover from this?* I was already thinking about the day I got out, and wondering how I was going to explain this mess because I didn't fully understand it myself. However, some people can't handle being behind bars at all, and this guy's mental condition was deteriorating as we sat there. I recall thinking that the officers and jail officials were not paying enough attention to how stressed and worried this man was. Obviously, some mistakes were made because while I was away being fingerprinted, the man used the end of a blanket to hang himself.

My friends, family and those who just knew me in Barberton were shocked by what had transpired. However, no one was more shocked than I was. The next morning I was charged with bank robbery because I had driven the would-be bank robber to the Bank on Wooster Road, located about five or six miles from where I grew up. Essentially, I was charged with being the get-away driver, even though I never actually helped anyone get away.

Just before police arrested me I had driven out of the parking lot because I was overwhelmed by the craziness of what I had become involved in. *What am I doing here?* I asked myself before exiting the lot. *I don't belong here. How did I get talked into this?*

I knew that an acquaintance intended to rob the bank when I dropped him off. However, I had no idea that the robbery had been foiled when I drove out of the parking lot. Only later did I learn that the would-be robber had been thwarted by a silent alarm. He had confronted an employee coming to work, and forced his way into the bank 20 minutes before the bank was to open at 9:00 a.m. He demanded that employees open the safe. Because the time lock on the vault had been compromised, the police received an alarm.

According to police reports, Barberton Officer Edward Wickwire was the first to arrive on the scene. When he exited his car, he slipped on ice and fell down. The would-be robber ran out of the bank, he controlled Wickwire at gunpoint and tried to re-enter the bank through the back door.

"When he found the self-locking door was closed, he tried to punch a hole in it and open it from the inside," Wickwire told the news agency *UPI*. "I grabbed (his) arm, managed to pull out my own pistol and fired three or four rounds at him."

Two of Wickwire's .38-caliber slugs had connected—wounding the robber once in the hand and once in the stomach. The robber had tucked $4,219 in cash into a suitcase before meeting up with the police officer.

Not knowing what had happened, I decided to leave the area and I was blocked by the police arrival just as I left the bank property.

More than three decades after my conviction, the question that still hangs over my head is why I became involved in this robbery. I had never before been involved in any crime. People who know me well will testify that this situation was out of character for me. The worst anyone could say about me before this day was that I had some impishness in me. I was like Eddie Haskell from the *Leave it to Beaver* show. In public, I was polite and well mannered. Behind the scenes, I stirred up some mischief. But the closest I ever came to an armed robbery before that moment was watching one on television.

The first admission about the events of January 17, 1975, is that I accept full responsibility for my role in the attempted robbery at a bank that was not far away from my childhood home. I knew what the man was going to do when I dropped him off. That is the truth, and I have had to live with that truth for 30 years. The price you pay isn't just the jail time. You carry the stigma for the rest of your life. To erase that stigma, you must have a spectacular accomplishment and even then your criminal record simply won't go away. My hope is that by telling my story maybe others will recognize the symptoms of depression and alcoholism that I was experiencing in 1975. If even one is spared the shame that I felt for my actions, then it will have been worth this exercise in self-examination.

Although the man that I drove to the bank has been identified in many articles through the years, he shall remain nameless in my book. He shall remain nameless because I refuse to allow him back into my world for even a moment. I will not give him any more notoriety than he has already received at my expense.

This is what I will say about him: he did play freshman football at the University of Michigan, although he wasn't much of a player. All of the Mellow Men were acquainted with him. However, none of us would have said he was a friend. We knew there was something unsavory about this man the first time we met. He dressed too well and he always drove a new Lincoln Continental. Each of us were always trying to put our nickels and dimes together to buy lunch. This guy always seemed to have plenty of money, and he didn't seem to have a regular job. We weren't sure how he accumulated his wealth, but we were confident it was a criminal enterprise.

In the fall of 1974, my football career was over and my mind was a hellish mix of sadness and anger. It was three years after my mother's death and yet my wounds, especially the pain in my heart, seemed fresh. The deaths of my relatives and former girlfriend, Valerie, played over and over in my mind like a repeating newsreel. I couldn't focus on anything. The Internal Revenue Service was seeking back taxes for the bonus I had received from the Falcons. I owed child support for my son Lewis Askew who was born when I was in high school. I had other loans to repay. My rage was escalating and the drinking and drug use was now central in my life. The devil was dancing on my soul and I was really walking on the outside borders of reality. Billy Taylor, the Michigan graduate, had disappeared. He had been replaced by an empty shell of a human being who didn't care what was happening around him. Knowing what I know now, I probably should have been hospitalized, or at least treated, for severe depression. However, I never sought professional help.

I preferred to self-medicate with drugs and alcohol. In December of 1974, I began to hang out with this former acquaintance. He had just finished a prison sentence. By then I knew what he was. Right after freshman football, he had gone to prison for robbery, credit card fraud and car theft. His most recent incarceration was over a parole violation.

He had money, and he was willing to pay to keep me high. That's all the reason I needed to stay in his company. It was too many years ago to provide an accurate timeline of when he suggested the robbery in Barberton, but I can swear on a Bible that it was his idea. He had been to Barberton once to meet a woman I had introduced him to, and I think he considered Barberton to be an easy mark for a bank robbery. He viewed Barberton as if it was Mayberry from the *Andy Griffith Show*. He didn't believe that a small town bank and police force would have the sophistication required to prevent this level of crime. The man who shall remain nameless acted as if he had some experience in bank robbery. To be honest, I'm not sure whether I believed he was actually going to follow through even when we drove to Barberton. I probably should have realized we were headed toward calamity when he insisted on stopping to purchase drugs and alcohol. He rarely drank or took drugs, but en route to Barberton he told me he knew "where to get the good stuff."

In hindsight, it's clear now that he wanted to keep me high all night to keep me under control. He knew me well enough to know that my history suggested that I wasn't easily pressured into doing something I didn't want to do. However, he probably didn't know that my depression left me more susceptible to coercion. When you are angry and shrouded in gloom every waking hour, any action is a possibility.

To me, the most significant piece of evidence to support my contention that I wasn't in my right mind when I was involved in this robbery is the mere fact that I was doing it in my hometown where I was extremely well known. I still had family in Barberton. In addition, the folks of Barberton had chipped in to send my mother to the Rose Bowl a few days before she died and 400 Barberton residents showed up at the Slovenian Center Hall to honor me on Billy Taylor Day. Even if I were considering a life of crime—which I was not—why would I launch that career in the place where everyone recognized me?

The night before the crime, we even stayed at a nearby Holiday Inn. How ridiculous is that? If I had really been thinking about this crime, would this have been what I would have done? It seems obvious that while my body was involved, mentally I wasn't anywhere near Barberton that day. That's why I think it felt like an out-of-body experience when the attempted robbery was going down. It was similar to how people describe near-death experiences. You are able to watch yourself.

I'm not trying to excuse the decision I made. I'm merely trying to explain why it occurred. Today I realize that I had been heading toward an eruption for three years. It could have manifested itself in many forms. I could have hit someone. I could have collapsed in a heap of tears. I could have driven my car off a bridge. What I did was involve myself in a bank robbery.

Driving to Barberton, I think I assumed the bank robbery scheme he had briefly discussed would evolve into a couple of days of womanizing and partying. The bank robbery plan just seemed like big talk to me.

But when he brought out his loaded gun in the hotel room I realized this was serious. I had never really been around guns.

"You ever shoot anybody?" he said in such a way to imply that he had.

At some point I said I wanted to call my family, and he pushed the gun barrel inches from my face and said, "It's too late to cop out now."

He kept aiming the gun in my direction, laughing and telling me stories about the different people he had hurt for "ratting him out."

"You had better be there when I come out of the bank because I know where your son and family live," he told me.

He repeated that often enough that the message was received even in my stoned and drunken haze. He kept insisting that I drink up, and I didn't need much encouragement in those days. To this day, I wonder what he had given me to smoke that night because I certainly understood what it was like to smoke marijuana. That was not like any marijuana I had ever smoked before. It was clearly laced with some other form of narcotic because I was out of my head quickly. I was the only one drinking out of the "special bottle" he had purchased. My vision was blurry. I'm convinced he was spiking my liquor as well.

"Let's get something to eat," I remember saying at one point, knowing that I was losing control of my senses.

The robbery mastermind rejected that idea. "You'll screw up your high and we're going to hit 'em in just a few hours."

He kept saying, "Your cut will be $20,000." When your mind is clouded in a drug-laced and depression-rooted fog, you don't focus on the criminal act. He made it seem like we were going to hit the lottery, not rob a bank. I was broke. I was depressed. I was high. My moral values and common sense did not come with me to that hotel room that night.

Most of my memories of that evening are hazy, but I have a clear memory of his insistence that I put my fingers on his gun.

He said he wanted me to know how the gun felt in my hand. I didn't want anything to do with his gun. Now I think he wanted to make sure my fingerprints were on that gun. I'm left wondering what his plans were had he successfully robbed that bank. Was he planning to pin the rap on me solely? Was he planning to do harm to me? I know that I thought he was a scary person.

We didn't really sleep a single minute that night, and the next morning he brought out a rubber ghoul mask that he said I had to wear "because it will make you look white."

Some of the final words he said to me were wrapped in a warning, "only punks and chumps get shot." That is either prophetic or ironic or both, considering he was the only person who ended up with bullet holes in his body.

Why didn't I run out of there? Why didn't I come to my senses? I can't answer that. The night at the Holiday Inn and the events of the next morning made it seem like I was living in an episode of the *Twilight Zone*. It was surreal. In my state, my mind didn't seem to be able to sort through the facts. I can tell you that I was thinking about bolting all the way to the bank that morning. Even after I dropped him off, I thought about driving away. Why didn't I? I can't tell you. I was obviously still high that morning, but the gravity of the situation was entering my awareness. I was regretting my actions even before I did them. Minutes before the police surrounded my car I was thinking, *How did I get involved with this character?* However, by then it was too late.

The whole episode, from the time I dropped off the would-be robber, until the time I was arrested probably took less than 25 minutes. It is amazing, when you think about it, that decisions made over such a short segment of my life have had three decades of consequences. In those 25 minutes, I went from Barberton's hometown hero to a source of embarrassment for the city's residents.

The night before, I thought it was silly when he had given me a rubber mask. Now that rubber mask, plopped on the seat next to me when I was arrested, was evidence of my involvement.

104

My brothers Jimmy and Thomas Jackson came down to the police station and my cousin Cleon Bibbs was there. I was too embarrassed to even speak much to them.

The real concern I had when I was arrested was the impact it would have on my son, Lewis Askew. I had become a father in 1968 when I was still in high school. Lewis lived with his mother in Barberton, and I was horrified to ponder the ridicule he would face as a result of his father being arrested for bank robbery.

Although I never carried a gun, entered the bank or participated in the actual robbery, the next day I was arraigned on the same federal bank robbery charges as the would-be robber faced. Under our law system, if you help the criminal, you are guilty of the crime. U.S. Magistrate Ralph Hartz set my bail at $50,000. The would-be robber had to be arraigned in the Barberton Citizen's Hospital where he was recovering from his wounds. I couldn't raise the money for the bail so I stayed in the Summit County Jail. The reality of my situation hit home when I was told that the maximum penalty for my offense was a 25-year sentence.

My understanding of what life would be like behind bars was also being brought home to me by my experiences at the Summit County jail. One morning I saw a prisoner take a serious beating over a doughnut. One prisoner had a doughnut, and another prisoner wanted that doughnut. "Set out that doughnut," he said. The owner refused and when the cell doors were opened for a daily exercise, four guys swooped in on the doughnut eater in his cell. He ended up on the ground, and those four guys beat him, kicked him, stomped on him. The victim laid there severely injured and his assailants calmly strolled away from the scene as if nothing had happened. It was as if they had just stopped to use the restroom. They just went about their business.

During my stay at the Summit County Jail, I was also interviewed about my knowledge of the robber's background and criminal ties.

"Do you know he has killed people?" the FBI agent asked me.

That level of questioning gets your attention. The FBI agent told me that my acquaintance had been suspected in other bank robberies. They asked me about his family and about whether I knew where he was hiding his money from the robberies. However, I really didn't know much of anything. This man was shrewd and manipulative. He wasn't sharing his innermost secrets with me. The truth is that he was just using me because I was convenient. Given my fondness for drugs and alcohol at the time, he probably viewed me as an easier mark than the bank

When Bo Schembechler heard about the situation, he immediately helped organize the raising of my bail money and money to hire a lawyer. Bo and my lawyer talked frequently.

The first meeting with Bo after he bailed me out was difficult. As I recall, Bo said simply, "Bill, what's going on down there? I can't believe this. People are calling and telling me these stories, and I can't believe it."

It was painful to talk to Bo under these circumstances. My respect for him was incalculable. It was as if I had shamed my father. Many turned away from me when I became involved in this crime, but Bo supported me. Butch Carpenter's dad Sam also supported me, helping me get a job in Flint at the Hurley Medical Center while I was out on bail. No matter who was in my corner, this wasn't going to go away. My attorney Gerald Gold told me early in the process, "You are going to have to do some time."

Another reason why I will not mention the would-be robber's name is that he tried to tell the authorities that the robbery was my idea. Healed from his wounds, he took the stand, he called the robbery attempt a "joint venture." He was obviously trying to make himself look less guilty by saying I talked him into this, even though he was the man who had been to prison three times. I was incensed that he tried to paint my involvement as being more than it was.

At my sentencing hearing, I had testified, "The involvement I had was very limited." My attorney told the judge that I shouldn't be considered "an everyday criminal."

"It's extremely unlikely that Billy Taylor will ever engage in any kind of criminal activity ever again," Gold said in the court proceedings, according to the *Akron Beacon Journal*.

My brother Jim kept telling me I should prepare myself to believe I was going to "do some time." However, in my mind, I was having a struggle to accept that notion. I kept believing probation was possible.

In the end, the robber and I received no leniency from the judge. On June 5, 1975, District Court Judge Leroy Conti , sentenced the robber to 12 years in prison, while I was given an 8-year sentence. When I heard the words, a shiver went down my spine. My attorney said my sentence was "normal" for this level of crime, but he also told the *Akron Beacon Journal* that he was surprised that my sentence was as long as it was, given my lack of criminal record.

My quote to the newspaper was, "The judge did what he thought was fair."

Obviously, the sentence was not what I believed to be fair. We had hoped that the judge would take into account that I had been a model citizen prior to this event. Apparently the judge wasn't swayed by the fact that I was a leader in the Fellowship of Christian Athletes, or that I had traveled to Vietnam to help entertain the troops, or that I held a degree from the University of Michigan. It didn't seem to matter to the judge that I had worked with disadvantaged youngsters in San Diego and Barberton, or that President Richard Nixon had invited me to the White House because of my athletic accomplishments and civic contributions. The common perception is that athletes often receive breaks in the legal system, but I don't believe that happened in my case. I think judges don't want to be perceived as giving favorable treatments to an athlete.

The only leniency I received from Judge Conti was there would be no minimum sentence imposed, which meant I was eligible for parole at any point in my sentence. In practical terms, it meant I would serve about one-third of my eight-year sentence.

My sentence was to be served at the Federal Correction Institution in Oxford, Wisconsin. The judge gave me time to get my life in order before I self-reported to prison.

It was probably at that time in my life that I understood what a caring man Bo is. Everyone would have understood if Bo chose not to associate with a man convicted of a felony. Remember, I had hurt him deeply by arguing with him on the sideline of the Coaches' All-American game. That resulted from a misunderstanding, but the hurt Bo felt was real. Remember also that Bo is from Barberton and he knew there would be people in my hometown that would have no sympathy for me. Many in the town were angry that I had brought shame to the city. There were people who wanted him to cut me loose. However, Bo is the kind of person who does what feels right in his heart, regardless of what other people say.

Bo organized my defense, and after the sentence was announced, Bo said he would accompany me on my journey to prison. Butch's father, Sam, also came.

Before I entered the prison in Oxford, Wisconsin Bo gave me some advice: "Everyone in prison is going to know you were an All-American and everyone is going to try to prove their toughness by coming after you. They are going to test themselves against you. You have to watch yourself in there."

Bo isn't just a good football mind. He analyzes every situation, on and off the field, correctly. He was absolutely right about what would happen to me in prison.

CHAPTER 9

INCARCERATION

THE REALITY OF A PRISON TERM DOESN'T arrive when the judge passes the sentence. The consequences of a criminal act becomes real when you walk down a long corridor and hear the main entrance jail door slam shut behind you. The degradation becomes undeniable minutes later as you stand naked while prison guards search your body cavities to make sure you aren't sneaking contraband into the prison population.

In preparation for my trip to the Federal Correctional Institution in Oxford, I had neatly folded t-shirts, underwear, vitamins, after-shave, and razors and placed them in a bag.

As soon as the check-in started, a guard dumped my vitamins in the trash and said, "You won't be needing these because they will be beyond the expiration date when you get out."

The other guards laughed. He threw out my after-shave and razors, and said my underwear weren't the right color or style. Essentially, there was nothing left in my bag when the check-in was complete.

The humiliation was just beginning. You are ordered to strip, and someone from the check-in looks into your mouth as you lift up your lips so they can check to see if you are hiding any contraband. They check under your tongue, and then the process gets worse. As part of the inspection, you are forced to lift up your testicles to make sure you haven't taped a joint to the underside and then you bend over and spread your cheeks to make sure you haven't created a makeshift storage area. Then you lift your feet and spread your toes. Every crevice of your body is inspected.

As I was going through this process, I recall thinking about how my experience seemed similar to what immigrants experienced as they entered America through Ellis Island. While I was a student at Michigan, I remember being horrified that immigration officials at Ellis Island would use metal hooks to lift the eyelids and examine the eyes of immigrants moving through the system. Anyone suspected of trying to enter the country with a disease, or mental illness, was marked with a letter on his or her clothing. It was just like you were a steer being inspected for auction. The treatment of immigrants was inhumane and insensitive. I had a better understanding of that after going through a prison check-in.

When the Oxford check-in procedure was completed, I knew I was no longer No. 42 Billy Taylor. I had become federal inmate number 00330-124.

Oxford is located in Central Wisconsin 60 miles north of Madison, and the drive out to the prison gave me some mental preparation for my incarceration. I don't know how that area is today, but back then the prison was isolated in a wooded, rural area. It seemed like we were in the wilderness. It seemed like the legal system was about to put you in a place where you could be forgotten. When you were imprisoned in Oxford and looked beyond the fences and guard towers, what you saw was a forest that didn't look enchanted. It looked eerie. The word among the prisoners was that the woods were overrun with bears, wolves, coyotes and colonies of snakes. Maybe that's what prison officials wanted us to think, and if that was their plan, it was effective.

Once we were sitting around talking about the isolation of the Oxford prison, and I said, "Hell, they could open the gates wide open right now, and I wouldn't walk out of this place." Everyone laughed. But that's how spooky it was out there.

Prison life is about survival. I was a strong, tough guy and I wasn't hassled often, but I had to fight early in my stay at Oxford to prove to everyone how rough I could be. I spent time in solitary confinement because of those fights. That's just the price that has to be paid to make sure the other inmates will leave you alone. Prison is just like the jungle. The lions and hyenas are all looking to prey on the weakest of the herd. Once you establish you are among the strongest of the pack, they will turn their focus elsewhere.

Initially, I had enough anger stored up that I allowed myself to get into verbal jousts with guards.

Early in my Oxford stay, my work detail duty included sweeping out the cell blocks and the cement walkways outside. One day, a guard made me sweep the grass. How are you going to sweep grass? He wanted me to police the area of cigarette butts. He was just trying to be cruel, just because he could.

It irritated me when a guard would break-up a card game, or would refuse to provide you with a pencil for writing a letter, because he wanted to punish you. The guard could have acted with kindness, but he chose to be a hard guy. This time I responded by screaming at him. I was in my cubicle when guards came down and handcuffed me and escorted me to solitary confinement.

"I'm already in prison, and you are going to lock me up on top of that—that's some crazy shit," I said to the guards.

However, I was smart enough to understand it was foolish to get drawn into a fist fight with a guard. There was a guy at Oxford named Jackson who was a decent fellow with a sad story. His story was that he had been a short-timer who had lost his temper and attacked a guard. When his trial was over, his six months had become 20 years.

What you discover quickly when you enter the federal penal system is that it is not about rehabilitation; it's about punishment. What you learn inside, is how to be a better criminal. Inmates were always talking about how to do crimes a little bit better and a little smarter so next time they wouldn't get caught.

In essence, prisons manufacture more highly skilled criminals. When I entered the prison system, I knew nothing about criminal enterprise. I didn't even know much about my crime of bank robbery because I never had been involved in the actual robbery. But by the time I left, I knew plenty about making money illegally. In prison, there is plenty of time to talk and little to talk about. It's not like at the end of the day, we could discuss how our career aspirations were going or how we were raising our kids. Inmates aren't usually talking about how they are going to polish up their resumes and pursue employment in computer sciences or the medical profession when they leave prison. The only networking an inmate can do from prison is talking with people who have everything from mayhem to murder on their resumes. I was one of the few prisoners at Oxford that owned a college degree.

Every day, inmates discuss their criminal experience. It was like every day I went to class for forgery, breaking and entering, drug dealing, money laundering, etc. By the time I was paroled, I knew 50 different ways to make money illegally. Obviously, that's not what inmates should be learning in prison, but that's the truth about life in the penitentiary. Also, when you are in prison, you have almost no opportunities to meet the kind of ambitious, solid citizens who will help you turn your life around. Criminals become your best friends. You need friends to survive in prison and those bonds can last beyond their prison stays. How many television shows have you watched when the detective says that two people came together to commit a crime because they had been cellmates in prison? When the police are trying to determine who a perpetrator worked with on a criminal act, the first direction they look at are those who went to prison with him.

When you are about to leave prison, inmates will tell you, "Look up this guy because he will help you out." They aren't usually directing you to their local minister.

My take on the situation was that the potential to do criminal activity is far greater after you leave prison than it was before you enter the system. It's not surprising to me that federal correctional institutions do plenty of repeat business.

Honestly, I didn't believe I would be in Oxford for very long. Remember my sentence left me immediately eligible for parole. The word was that the parole board would be convening a few months after I arrived at Oxford. My presumption was that the parole board would look favorably on the fact that I had no previous brushes with the law before this conviction. I also had that history of community service. Moreover, Bo Schembechler was in my corner and Michigan's United States Senator Donald Riegle wrote a letter of support for me.

Nevertheless, the five-person parole board came in, mentioned that I had some letters of support, and then voted that my parole request be denied. Obviously, the eligibility for early parole is written into the law to help somebody, but it wasn't me. The whole process was over in minutes. Apparently, I wasn't rich enough or well connected enough to receive full consideration. Even though on paper I looked like an ideal candidate for quick release, I had the sense that the parole board never seriously considered my request.

That news flattened my emotions like they had been run over by a steamroller. However, it forced me to begin thinking in terms of serving the 30 months that was likely for someone with an eight-year sentence. Other inmates advised me to break off contact with female friends outside. "You don't want to be living in a fantasy world," the guys would tell me. "All we have in here are asses and elbows."

It became clear that I needed to keep busy to maintain my sanity.

"Do the time," one inmate told me. "Don't let the time do you."

That's when I began to write poetry. I now have a significant number of poems, and the majority of them were penned while I was in prison.

One of my favorite poems is entitled "*Reality Must Be Realized Everywhere*." It was written three days after Christmas in 1977 after I had formed an opinion of the prison experience.

Here I am in a place where is no room for likes, dislikes and emotions. I find myself subject to all kinds of notions because I am primarily surrounded by too much commotion!

I could say I'm lonely or apprehensive or possibly just a little afraid.

But, those are all emotions and here there is no place for things like that.

At times, I feel lost but there is nothing pertaining to misdirection because I've been here quite a while and movement is quite limited.

Nor is my situation of being lost pertaining to where I'm going or why I'm here.

If that were my situation, I'd feel some fear but there is no place for that in here!

I do know that I'm tarrying some place close to hell but not just because there is always the presence of a cell. Cells are material and visible. These things are not hard to deal with. It is the invisible and the spiritual things that battle the day and the night and crosses you because you exist from one to another.

The tendency it seems is that if you are "Bourgeois" which I am not, you'd better start to make some noise, and if you are quiet within, your fellow members prefer you don't wear a grin. I'm humble and I love, but now it is kept "boxed" inside and stored up for later on for such things are out of place here within. Here I don't have sisters, parents, nor brethren

I love each day anyway. I love to think of doing what I'd love to be doing that is, but there is a time for everything and a reason that also means that sometimes loving to hate has a season too; I know for everything there is a time because right now from my enemies I must step aside, but while smiling I'm hating to watch this detailed plan of genocide.

I am strong but I am chained. I can talk but dare not speak. I can act but I dare not though, I cannot error because the wrong one means I'm through; But, loved ones do not worry because only emotions can cause a mistake while caught in this hell. But there is no room for emotions here where I dwell and I can adapt because I must; After-all, the decisive factor of whether we live or exist is dependent upon how well we adapt!

Yes, I am the person described and determined as driving steel that I shall not allow my humility to become "lost" during this still, but I have had to program because my hand in the lions' mouth, I dare not move too fast or shout too loud, but believe me I got my teeth gritted; but there is more, much more of me than this, but I am only what I must be here where I presently exist, But until later I shall box this season in me too, because where you are that type of person does need to exist unless there are no likes, dislikes nor emotions there! Is there? Reality must be realized everywhere.

Celebrity status in prison has mixed consequences. I suspect it earned me at least one benefit that Bo escorted me to prison. I believe the guards had considerable respect for Bo. I think that helped me land a desirable job as a clerk for the captain of the guards. That work assignment gave me access to a typewriter, which certainly was beneficial for my writing. Also it was a good job, with the right balance of busy work and free time. I answered phones, typed memos and delivered the inner-office mail around the prison.

I walked the same route every day to deliver mail to various venues around the prison, and I could see the path I was wearing down on the grounds. It reminded me of the path that a dog wears out along the fence line when he is penned up in the backyard. The outside aspect of my job allowed me to have a vision of the changing of the seasons. That simply reminded me that life was moving on while I was behind bars. I, in response wrote, "winter brings the cold, yet lovely snow, spring time warms the heart, but makes me glow. Summer greens the grass, clears the sky, autumn browns the leaves and quickly passes by."

Just as Bo had predicted, guys came after me to measure their toughness against an All-American running back. I was smart enough to realize that I shouldn't be involved in any prison athletic leagues. Whatever happened on the field would eventually result in problems for me. However, inmates were always harassing me about playing in the flag football league. To be honest, I wasn't in the mood for football, even if it had just been for fun and games. Plus, what did I have left to prove athletically?

Eventually my decision not to play evolved into an issue about my toughness. One guy came up and said he had played some football here or there, and suggested that I was "scared to go on the field" against him.

"You wouldn't be able to compete out there," he said to me.

On the inside, when guys call you out, you have to deal with those issues. Otherwise, you will be labeled as a sissy or a chump, and eventually you will be jumped because of that.

I played two games in the Oxford Flag Football League—just long enough to rough up a couple of dudes. I just ran into those guys like I was running against Ohio State. I knocked the hell out of them because they had no idea what they were doing. A few years before, I had been hit by Ohio State's Jack Tatum and Jim Stillwagon in full gear. I certainly had no difficulty plowing through prison league jocks.

This was supposed to be non-contact football. To bring down a runner, you just had to grab his flag. However, one dude tried to come in low and take out my legs. Back when I was Michigan's starting tailback, when a defender would try to chase me out of bounds I would lower my shoulder and take him on. I would punish him for his effort to tackle me.

That's what I did to this inmate. I lowered my shoulder and drove him mercilessly into the ground. He lost a tooth or two, and he was bleeding. When the play was over, I stood up and looked directly at him. I called him a "sucker." No one bothered me about playing sports again.

Interestingly, one of my buddies in prison was Hayward Brown, who had gained considerable media attention because he had been involved in a high profile police killing.

Brown and two other men, John Boyd and Mark Bethune, became caught up in a shoot-out with Detroit police. Some police officers were killed and the three young men escaped. A national manhunt followed. I don't profess to know what really happened, but there were those in the black community at the time who believed that the three men were defending themselves because they believed the police intended to kill them. Before the shoot-out, the three were wanted for robbing drug dealers. Cops in Atlanta eventually killed Boyd and Bethune. Brown was eventually captured, but he was represented by noted attorney Ken Cockrel and acquitted. Prosecutors stayed after Brown on other charges and eventually he ended up at Oxford.

One of the inmates would ask Hayward whether he had actually shot a policeman. "That's what they say I did," Hayward would reply.

No one ever admits to any crime in prison. Everyone is innocent. When folks would ask me about my crime, I would say, "They say I robbed a bank."

You could never be sure whether an inmate was telling you the truth or not. Much of the time an inmate lied about why he was even in the joint. Often a prisoner would exaggerate his offenses to make himself seem tougher. Or, sometimes he had committed a crime he didn't want us to know about. For example, a child molester isn't going to want to discuss his crime. We called prison conversations "jail tails" because you didn't have any idea whether you were listening to fact, fiction, fable or fairytale.

Brown really did become a close friend. He schooled me on the ways of prison. He told me which guards to avoid and how to take advantage of the few privileges we had. He was the jailhouse lawyer. He was a very smart man who spent much of his free time reading law books in the prison's law library. He showed me how I could apply for a transfer to the prison in Milan, Michigan, to "re-establish ties with my family" and to "continue my education."

Our transfers were approved and we both ended up at Milan, which was located just a 14-minute drive from the University of Michigan campus. Everyone was aware in Milan that we were buddies, and no one wanted to mess with us.

People can say Hayward was a bad dude, but he was never like that around me. He was a good friend. In fact, even though paroled felons aren't supposed to associate with other felons, we did see each other socially after Hayward was paroled. However, he was killed during a drug deal that went sour around 1984.

Once I transferred to Milan, my prison life was improved dramatically because I became eligible for the work-study program. To be eligible you had to be a model prisoner, and in hindsight I realize that it was fortunate that all but one of my fights with other inmates had occurred off the books. They had been started, finished and we had moved on before guards had known that they occurred. I might not have been eligible for this program had I come to Milan with five prison fights on my record.

Bo then helped me get enrolled in graduate school as part of a work-study program that was already in place at Milan.

Shortly after I arrived at the Milan Federal Corrections Institution, Warden Hanberry called me into his office and said he wanted me to be "his boy."

I initially didn't say much in response because I really didn't know how to interpret what he was saying. Was he asking me to be his flunky or a snitch? I certainly wasn't going to be a snitch. In the prison community, snitch ranks below the cockroach in terms of the social strata, and a cockroach might have a longer life expectancy than a snitch in a prison setting.

Right away, I think he realized that it was a poor phrasing for a white authority figure to be asking a black man to be his "boy." He said immediately he didn't mean "anything negative" by his word choices. He was simply trying to ask me to be a model citizen, someone he could hold up as a positive example of how productive an inmate can be. A celebrity prisoner within the system can be a large positive or negative factor, depending on how that prisoner behaves. I think Hanberry was just trying to size me up. Over the months we actually became friends, I thought he was a good man, and a fair person. If I made requests that were within the rules, Hanberry usually granted those requests.

It took me 10½ months of being a full-time student to finish my master's degree in adult and continuing education. I was an 'A' student and I earned some credits toward my Ph.D. Hanberry was proud that I was the first Milan prisoner to earn a master's degree while still in prison.

If there is any program in the prison system that does further help a prisoner prepare for the outside world, this was it. My last year in prison was quite palatable. I even had some weekend church furloughs—giving me two days away from the prison. I wasn't just a student. I also had a job. I worked for Dr. Charles Moody in Michigan's Office of Educational Opportunities. I was already dating—if you can call it that considering I was in prison—a woman who would eventually become my wife and the mother of my three children, William III, Alden and Mariah. We are divorced today, she has asked me not to identify her in this book, and I am honoring that request. But at that time I was in the work study program she already had earned her master's degree as well and I was beginning to think we would be married and have a good life together.

Before I started work on my master's at Michigan, my lady had bought me some nice clothes to wear to class. Each morning, before I left for school, I could change from my prison issues into regular street wear. When I left for school, I was able to look like a normal human being. After the checkout procedure, the prison van would drop me off on campus. There was another inmate working on an undergraduate degree, and some others who were being dropped off for work. We had a designated time when we had to return to a specific location to be picked up by the van. It was real trouble if we weren't there. Since I was working on a master's degree, I needed considerable time in the library and sometimes I didn't have to be picked up until seven or eight o'clock at night. Very few people on campus knew I was an inmate at Milan. Once on campus, I was allowed to go and come as I pleased. I had money deposited to my account because I was working. I could eat lunch at McDonald's, or browse the bookstore, as long as I was where I needed to be for my pick-up.

Although my life was improved at Milan, primarily because of my educational opportunities, it was far from ideal.

My fighting days weren't completely over when I moved from Oxford to Milan. I had been assigned to teach English and Writing at the prison and I was serious about that pursuit because I contemplated teaching when I got out of prison. I ran my classroom just like it would have been managed in a real school. Not all of the prisoners appreciated a tightly run classroom. One day while I was teaching, an inmate was disrespectful and I had him removed. After class, he confronted me. There was an exchange of words and he swung at me. I swung back. He was a big man, and when my punch landed, he went down like a sack of potatoes. I proceeded to beat the hell out of him. I think I hurt him badly. I didn't know for sure because I scooted away so I didn't have my privileges taken away. It's not a pretty story, but it is the reality of the system. You often had to defend yourself in prison. I didn't know if he had a shank. I had less than a year to go in my sentence and I knew that I did not want to spend the next 12 months looking over my shoulder because he might be ready to jump me. If you didn't accept a challenge, you would be viewed as soft or weak. If you carried that label, you were abused by a multitude of people.

My scariest moment in Milan actually involved a legal hearing and not a physical assault.

Jealousy is a problem in the prison environment, particularly when you have some inmates receiving privileges and others who are not. When I was in the work-study program at Milan, it was made clear to me that there were some prisoners with lengthy sentences who were quite jealous that I was able to get up every morning and leave prison life behind for 10 hours.

Inmates were constantly asking me to smuggle contraband back into the prison for them. "Are you nuts?" I would say. "I'm not going to risk losing these privileges."

Undoubtedly, some of them weren't happy with that answer. With six months left in my sentence, guards discovered a marijuana joint hidden in either the towels or bed linen in my cubicle. I can't say for sure where they found it because I did not put it there. I have not been a saint in my life when it comes to drug use, but in this instance, I was completely innocent. I had too much at risk. I wasn't using drugs in prison. That essentially was my defense.

A hearing was scheduled and I was frightened because there was much at stake here. I could have lost my privileges, or worse. I could have been charged with drug possession. If convicted I could have ended up with an extended sentence.

Fortunately, I had some factors in my favor. The chaplain and my caseworker both supported me in my contention that I had been framed. Secondly, prison officials were well aware that inmates planted contraband in other prisoners' cells.

I was convinced that somebody was trying to bring me down, because after the hearing was scheduled, another inmate said, "They got your ass now."

However, it was entirely possible that it wasn't a framing at all. The marijuana could have been placed in my cubicle by someone trying to dump it because he suspected his cubicle was about to be searched. The prison set-up at Milan isn't like what you see on television. There was no sliding gate that closed at the end of each night. We all had our own cubicles that were always open. To picture it, just think of a line of lavatory stalls without any doors on them. Anyone could come into your room at any time. Prison officials knew that some prisoners would actually hide their illegal goods in someone else's room and hope to reclaim it at another time.

When it came time for me to make my defense, I said simply, "Why would I risk all that I have going to have one joint in prison?"

The hearing panel believed me, probably because they wanted to believe me. In those situations, it's really just your reputation that is on trial. If I had been a troublemaker or a mouthy prisoner, I probably would not have been believed. I was doing well in school. However, in hindsight, it's still frightening for me to remember that my future was in the hands of people who could have kept me in prison for a much longer time just because someone didn't like me. I'm confident that some innocent men have had rulings go the wrong way for them because their personality rubbed officials the wrong way.

As much as I enjoyed the freedom of being allowed out of the prison for educational purposes, I despised the degradation of the strip search that was required each time I returned. It didn't become less humiliating just because you went through it every day. It's difficult to balance the emotional swings that accompany being free for half the day and imprisoned for the rest.

After leaving prison, I once described the situation to a reporter this way, "You're a person for those certain hours two or three days a week. Then you go back to prison and you have to behave like an animal. If you go back there and try to act like a person, then people there take aggressive action to make you behave like an animal."

In Milan, I also met inmate Daniel Savickas, who had some connection to Students for a Democratic Society (SDS) and knowledge of what had happened with those who were involved with the Chicago Seven Trial. It was a treat to end up as his cellmate because he was the first man in the prison I met that shared my interest in politics. We shared the same sentiment that the legal system was in major need of reform.

Again, I want to reiterate that I did not consider myself guilt free. I accepted full responsibility for my actions regarding the bank robbery. I did indeed have prior knowledge what the would-be robber's intentions were in Barberton. However, I felt the punishment was more severe than it needed to be. When I looked around Oxford and Milan, the multitude of black faces suggested to me that the judicial system was not really blind. It was definitely not colorblind. Savickas and I spent many hours discussing the hypocrisy of those who praised the merits of our judicial system and then did nothing to fix the inequality that existed within that system. Both Savickas and I were feeling rebellious in those days and we were thankful to find someone who followed that same line of reasoning.

You adjust to not seeing your old friends and family, but the worst aspect of prison for me was not having contact with my son, Lewis Askew. I went two years without seeing him. The interesting aspect of our letter writing is that he never asked me to explain why I was going to prison. We wrote letters, and what I remember most about those letters was that he was worried about how I was. To him, it didn't seem to matter that I was in prison. I could have been in the army somewhere or working out of the country. His focus was just on whether I was doing okay.

Once released I was still infuriated about the fact that I couldn't see my son for two years. "How in the hell will keeping you separated from your son make you a better person?" I said to a reporter. "That was just another inhumane aspect of the whole penal system."

Not many of my memories about prison are treasured, but one is. While I was at Milan, boxer Muhammad Ali visited the facility. Warden Hanberry arranged for me to have a special meeting with one of the greatest athletes the world has ever known.

Ali had a grin on his face when he shook my hand. "The Warden tells me that you are the baddest man in the whole prison," he said.

He raised his fists in a boxing pose. "Well, I'm the baddest man in the whole world," he said laughing

My dukes were raised, and Ali fired a couple of jabs in the air around me. His hands were like lightning. I was in awe.

When I was released from prison on October 17, 1977, it was like I was suddenly breathing pure oxygen. Freedom is always best enjoyed after it has been taken away. With a master's degree in hand, I had a job with General Motors within a couple of weeks of release.

Those managing the federal prison system probably would have viewed me as a successful rehabilitation, but the truth is that I was rehabilitated the moment I committed the crime. I didn't need prison to convince me I would never do that again.

If anything, what prison did for me is help me embrace a deeper conviction for my growing belief that a black man plays the game of life on an uneven playing field. African Americans make up only about 12 percent of the population in the United States, but they seem to be taking up the majority of prison cells. I've seen statistics that suggest that a black male faces a 30 percent chance of going to jail in his lifetime.

A curious aspect of my felony conviction is that my white friends always were looking for me to explain my involvement in the bank robbery, while my black friends never asked why I did it.

"It's been a difficult thing to explain to white friends," I told the *Akron Beacon Journal* eight months after my release. "Most blacks feel that when you're black, you're born in jail. That's something totally foreign to my white friends and acquaintances. Prison didn't make me feel more black. It made me feel more confined."

Certainly, I had an awareness of racial inequality before prison, but my stay there refined my thinking on the issue. More than 25 years later, after another major rise and fall, I would make constructive use of my feelings and observations in the educational world in the form of a doctoral thesis on the disadvantages that minority students face in the world of education.

When I walked out of that prison, I was proud because I had furthered my education while doing my time. However, more importantly I was proud because I had survived. I had been knocked down, and I had gotten back up. It was as if Bo was still my coach. He told me to be strong and I was strong. I had done the time. The time had not done me. Upon my exit, I was confident that my life was back on course. Sure, I had done some fighting in prison, but I also had done some praying. I had made peace with the Lord. I understood that the anger I felt towards Him after the death of my mother was misplaced. Today I realize how I was able to re-connect with God during my time in prison because years later I would need a miracle to save my life. And I found out that God was there for me.

CHAPTER 10

THE MIRACLE

ALDEN "BUTCH" CARPENTER, THE MELLOW Man with maturity beyond his years, died way too young.

He was 28, a picture of health, playing pick-up basketball at the Michigan Intramural Building, when he collapsed and died on February 2, 1978. He had sprinted out of bounds to reclaim a loose ball when he suddenly fell to the floor. The family learned that Butch suffered from an undiagnosed congenital heart problem. He was survived by his wife Vivian.

Even with all of the tragedies I had endured over the past six years of my life, Butch's death was the most difficult for me to accept. How could the cleanest living member of our group be dead before his 30th birthday? That wasn't just my thought. All of the Mellow Men gathered for his funeral and we all felt the same way. Butch lived a healthy lifestyle in both mind and body. When we were all living together, Butch was the one guy among us who wasn't obsessed about when the next party would be held or who the next girl would be in his life. Even at 19 and 20 years old, he was thinking about the big picture. This is a kid who was a good enough athlete to start for Michigan. I recall that he had a sack against Stanford in the 1972 Rose Bowl. However, he was also an accomplished student. At the time of his death, he had already been working as an accountant and just entered Michigan's Law School.

When we were all struggling to find the words to pay homage to Butch, Thom Darden summed up Butch's life better than anyone else did.

"Nothing came easy for Butch and that's what I admired about him," Thom said. "He wasn't the greatest athlete. He wasn't the smartest person in the classroom. He wasn't the guy with the most charisma. But he put it all together through hard work. And he succeeded in all of those areas. He succeeded on the field. He succeeded in the classroom. He succeeded with other human beings. He was a great example for us. He was a very caring man."

It's natural when someone dies young to wonder why you have been spared and he has died. I certainly had reason to be particularly humbled by Butch's death. He had lived life the right way, always embracing a Christian lifestyle, and he was now dead. I had danced with the devil on occasion, and I was still alive. Remembering how the would-be robber had pointed the gun at me the night before the bank robbery, it wasn't hard for me to wonder why God had spared me. Was there a reason that God still needed me on this earth?

Butch Carpenter was an inspirational human being. At that time of his death, I think I probably believed that I owed it to Butch's memory to make something out of my life. While my intentions were good, it has taken me years to live up to my desire.

In 1978, I was married, thinking about building a family, and holding down a job at General Motors. I believed I had my life on line for success and prosperity. I was wrong. After I was laid off in 1980, I became more involved with alcohol. I did some student teaching, but I didn't truly push for a career. My former wife was highly educated and earning a very good wage. She made enough to support us. I would watch the children while she worked, and then I would want to go out and enjoy the nightlife. Not surprising, after a while, our marriage deteriorated to the point that she didn't want me in the house.

At some stages of my disease, I made efforts to clean up my act. On March 24, 1989, the Exxon Valdez grounded on Bligh Reef, and dumped almost 11 million gallons of oil into the biologically rich waters of Prince William Sound. I heard that Exxon was paying up to $2,000 per week to help with the clean up, and I traveled to Alaska to get the job. I witnessed the ecological devastation first hand. I saw wildlife covered in oil…dying. I earned good money and sent it back home, but I didn't slay my demons. When I had days off, I drank, even though we were being drug-tested before we went back on the ship.

My last major effort to clean up my life came in 1995 when I went through a rehabilitation program at Share House, and went six months without using. You are supposed to attend 90 Alcohol Anonymous meetings in 90 days. I attended 120 in 90 days. I was making a serious effort. While at Share House, I met Father Markham. He knew my entire story and said, "I can use someone like you."

He was in charge of East Catholic High School, near the Warren and Gratiot area. It was a school that had gone from being a white school to being a predominantly black school and he wanted a minority assistant principal, with the idea that the assistant would become the principal within a year's time.

The job went well for a few months. It seemed as if I was restoring my life. I purchased a new car, and rented a decent place to live in Harper Woods. I had my children over for barbecues several times.

I thought I had licked my addiction. But one payday the devil in me came back to life. I had about $1,500, and something inside me said, "Have a drink, you deserve it."

I bought one beer at a convenience store and drank that. Then I stopped at a bar, and ordered a double scotch with a beer chaser. I hadn't felt that warm flush feeling that comes with hard liquor in a long time. It felt real good, too good. I started thinking about all of the women I had partied with on the streets. I thought about throwing a party at my house in Harper Woods. That's what I did. Drugs and alcohol flowed. We were up all night. I didn't go to work the next day. I didn't call in. I took the phone off the hook.

Father Markham came to my house but I didn't answer the door. Women and addicts were still partying in my place. I looked through the peephole, and I could hear Father Markham saying: "You are an assistant principal; you can't just not show up for work." I felt terrible for letting him down, but not enough to shake me out of my relapse.

Some people reached out to me, trying to get me re-focused on a clean life. Butch Carpenter's brother Brian had experienced some problems and had straightened out his life. He was the first to call. Our conversation went like this:

"What's going on BT?"

"Nothing, everything is cool."

"You using again?"

"Everything is all right."

"You can't be blowing this job."

"No, everything is all right."

Then I hung up. I never went back to that job. I never saw Father Markham again. I lost my car and my place in Harper Woods. I found a temporary job as a laborer. I rented another apartment, but lost that within 60 days. That's when I moved permanently onto the streets, living primarily out of an abandoned house in the area of Lakewood and Jefferson, in Detroit. Every once in a while, someone would illegally hook-up some electricity for a day or two. But primarily we were without utilities. In the winter, when the temperature would dip down to zero or below, I would wrap myself in every piece of clothing I owned. Having survived winters on the streets, I'm amazed that more homeless people don't perish in December, January and February.

Instead of using my education for gainful employment, I was just using my cunning to survive. Instead of hanging out with the Mellow Men, I was hanging out with guys named Skinny Pimp, Mad Dog and Bull Dog. To them, I was just another homeless addict named Bill. I never once revealed that I was Billy Taylor, the former All-American from the University of Michigan. I was embarrassed by what I had become, but when you are an addict, you can't locate the exits from the life you are living.

Once on the streets, I hooked up with a prostitute named Denise. Everyone called her Little Bit. She was a petite, feisty young woman from a good home. Her parents still lived nearby and she returned home occasionally to clean up and get some food. However, she was an addict. She would turn a trick and then she and I would spend the money on drugs. She was my girl on and off. To be honest, I had great affection for her. She was a spirited fighter. She wouldn't allow herself to be pushed around. We argued all the time, but we took care of each other. When we weren't together, I missed her. It makes it easier to survive on the street when you have someone looking after you.

To survive on the streets you actually must have some measure of organization. It takes some scheming and planning to feed your habit and to keep yourself safe. I was always thinking about ways to earn a few dollars for some food. Some of the elderly people in the area would give me a couple of dollars and some food for shoveling their driveway. Although I drank and drugged every day, I worried about my security. When I lived in the abandoned house, I would push an old freezer in front of the door before I went to sleep just so I would have some warning if someone came in.

Food stamp day was party day on the street. Homeless people qualify for food stamps. We were all excited about every food stamp day because we knew we could convert our food stamps into cash and turn the cash into liquor and drugs. We called it "busting stamps." If you received $80 in food stamps, you could hang out at a grocery store and sell them for $35 or $40 if you were lucky. As soon as you made that transaction, you headed straight to the dope house. You would be hungry, but you would bypass every grocery store and McDonald's, to make sure you could spend every cent on drugs.

Eating is not a No. 1 priority for an addict, but I had a plan when I needed food. I figured out when Kentucky Fried Chicken would throw out the food that they didn't sell each day. I would try to be waiting at the backdoor when the employee was going to the dumpster. If I got there on time, the guy would recognize me and just hand me the bag. If I missed the hand-off, I would have to dig the food out of the trash bin.

The owner of a convenience store on the corner of Lakewood and Jefferson also allowed me to trade my labor for liquor, an occasional sandwich and a few bucks. In winter, I shoveled snow. In the summer I swept and mopped the store.

In my homeless years I was arrested more than 20 times, always for petty offenses like vagrancy, or possession of drug paraphernalia or disturbing the peace.

The police who patrolled that area all knew me. I would be standing on the corner, with the pimps, hookers and other addicts cursing the officers as they went by. They were accustomed to verbal volleys with me. Obviously, I was angry, and I had never really addressed the depression that had hounded me since the 1970s.

"Get off the corner Bill Taylor," an officer would say.

"Why don't you get off the corner," I would say.

"All right, you'd better be careful," the officer would reply.

"Or what? Don't you have anything better to do than harass us? Why don't you go find some real criminals?" I would say.

I knew how far to push the officers without getting arrested. Clearly, my hostility would show during my verbal jousts with police officers. Honestly, there were nights when I didn't mind getting locked up. If it was a cold night, a warm cell with a sandwich seemed inviting. I knew I would only be in jail for a night or two. By Detroit standards, I wasn't much of a criminal. I didn't have a gun or a knife and I hadn't shot or cut anyone. I was Mr. Misdemeanor. The longest I ever spent in jail for my so-called crimes was about three weeks.

The most amazing aspect of my days on the street is that I suffered from no illnesses nor picked up any diseases. I had no hospital stays and only suffered one injury that needed treatment. One day another addict stole a phone booth and he asked me to help him search the coin box for money. Armed with a hammer, my plan was to use a spike as a chisel to break open the box. Unfortunately, I missed the spike with the hammer and gouged my hand severely. Blood was everywhere. I was forced to walk to the hospital for stitches and a tetanus shot. Hospitals can't turn away indigent patients.

One night, a gang of eight men encircled me and beat me severely. I hadn't done anything, they were just pimps and drug dealers having some fun. Fortunately, I didn't suffer any broken bones, just a swollen face and severe bruises. My attitude about fighting was strike quickly and run. I still could run. My attitude: run and live to fight another day. Even in a drunken state, I was careful. I didn't even like going to the drug houses to buy drugs because I didn't want to get busted. I would send someone else, but they were usually addicts themselves and they would steal half your drugs.

Eventually I had to start going myself. I remember one time I was buying drugs and I recognized an undercover cop. "I wouldn't by the stuff," he said. "They have better stuff on the next street."

Then he whispered that the place would be busted soon. I left and ran down the alley. Later that day, the place was raided.

By 1997 my alcohol and drug tolerance was amazingly high. I could down a fifth of hard liquor with a beer chaser and smoke marijuana and not be falling down drunk. I would be high, but I wouldn't be throwing up, or sick, or staggering. I could function with that level of alcohol in my system. Given my tolerance, I wonder now how far away I was from death on the streets. How long could I have continued to drink like that? I have no answers because God reached down and saved me on August 17, 1997.

There are those who will not want to believe the details of this story. But I know that I was saved by a miracle on that day. It was a true miracle.

Around 5:00 that morning, after walking all night, I settled into a porch of an abandoned, boarded-up building in the Lakewood and Jefferson area. Always worried about security, I had surveyed the grounds before settling in to finish my liquor. There was nobody around. I remember I was starting to think about where I was going to go that morning to scrounge up a few dollars for more liquor.

Without warning, a voice said strongly, "William Taylor come forth."

Startled by the disruption of the morning calm, I jumped straight in the air and my vodka tumbled out of my hand. I tried to grab it before it shattered on the cement, but I missed. When the bottle broke, I was filled with anger. The death of good liquor was a tragic event for an addict.

"Damn it," I yelled and immediately got up with the thought of pounding someone for the interruption of my solitude.

I did a reconnaissance patrol around the area, checking the alley, the weeds and high grass, and realized quickly that there was no one anywhere around the area. When I returned to the porch and I sat down I was overwhelmed by a spiritual feeling.

"God, is that you?" I said.

I didn't wait for an answer because I knew it had been God. I was scared, shaking violently. I rose from the porch and began quick-stepping toward Jefferson Avenue. I didn't stop when I reached Jefferson. Without looking for traffic, I marched into the middle of the road. At that hour of the morning, the traffic was light, but there were cars coming in both directions and none hit me. I crossed over and started east on Jefferson, not having any idea where I was going or why I was even walking. When I crossed Lakewood I looked down the street and saw the red van owned by a woman who had been kind to me in previous encounters. She hired me a few times to do work around her home. She paid well for that neighborhood. Some people would pay you $5 to shovel their driveway and walkway, and you accepted that fee because you were desperate. She usually paid $15 or $20. However, I kept going down Jefferson for several more minutes before it occurred to me that I should turn around and head back toward that red van. At the time, I remember being hungry and it made sense that maybe I could get some work at the house with the red van.

The woman was Sheryl Carson, although at the time I did not know who she was. She owned Family Tyes, a company that operates Adult Foster Care homes in the Detroit area. I just knew she was a kind lady who hired me and would occasionally wave at me if she saw me on the streets.

All the time I walked that morning, I kept looking over my shoulder because I was scared out of my mind. Hearing directly from God is not an everyday occurrence. However, even before I knew how this miracle would unfold, I knew God had contacted me. I was sure of that.

By the time I got back to the house with the red van, it was almost 8:00 in the morning, or near that time. When you are living on the streets, time has less relevance in your life. I saw Miss Carson and asked her for a job. I wasn't healed quite yet because I was now thinking that the money would go to liquor and that would help calm me down.

"As a matter of fact," she said, "I need the grounds cleaned up around here."

When I finished the work she handed me $15, and asked me if I wanted to come to one of her other homes, off Mack, and do some landscaping. A ton of dirt had been delivered the day before, and she needed the yard leveled and shrubs planted. I walked about 15 miles per day because that's the only way I could get around. I often did manual labor for my money. I didn't steal anyone's money or sell drugs. She could tell by looking at me that I could handle the job.

"Are you going to pay me?" I asked.

"Of course—how much do you want?"

"Fifty dollars," I said, not knowing why I chose that amount.

She agreed and soon she was driving me over to the house near Grosse Pointe. Later I would find out that house was controversial because police officers lived in that neighborhood. It was a bit more affluent in that area and the residents didn't want the group home there. Sheryl had received threatening letters.

During the car ride, I must have seemed nervous and quiet, because Miss Carson asked me a couple of times whether I could work. I kept insisting I was fine, but in my mind, I was trying to sort out my meeting with the Almighty. There was a huge pile of dirt when I arrived and I moved about half of it in just under an hour. I was throwing this dirt 20 or 30 feet at a time. I was working at a Herculean pace. I never felt stronger in my entire life.

While I was shoveling, Sheryl Carson and her friend Miss Lydia came outside and sat at a table on the porch to drink lemonade. They were talking about Miss Carson's desire to hire a teacher for her group homes to provide her clients with some basic education in math and English.

In all of the time I had spent on the street, I had never once revealed my educational background to anyone.

I stuck my shovel in the dirt, and said, "Miss Carson I can teach your clients." I couldn't believe what I was saying, even after I opened my month.

She was obviously surprised to hear me speak. "Mr. Taylor, you say you can teach my clients? What credentials do you have?" she replied.

"I have a Master's Degree from the University of Michigan," I said.

Miss Carson peered over her glasses like she had just heard me deliver a whopper of a lie. She was staring at a man with mattered hair and dirty shorts. I probably hadn't had a shower in months.

"Can you prove that?" she asked.

"I think I can. I think Michigan will send me a transcript," I answered.

She invited me immediately into the house to use the telephone. By then it was past noon, I hadn't had anything to drink for eight hours. With the hard labor thrown in, I had sobered up. I made the call, but when the Michigan receptionist asked for an address to send the transcript I had none to provide.

"Send it to my group home," Miss Carson said.

When the telephone call was made, I went back to shoveling the dirt. However, Sheryl Carson was not done talking to me. Our conversation went like this:

"Can I ask you a question, Mr. Taylor?"

"Yes, M'am."

"If you have a Master's Degree from the University of Michigan, why are you shoveling my dirt?"

"Because I drink too much and I get high too much."

"At least he's honest," Miss Lydia said.

Miss Carson still had one question that had to be asked.

"I don't allow any alcohol or drugs in my facilites," she said. "Can you get clean?"

I put down my shovel again. "Yes, I can," I said, probably not believing it at the time because I didn't fully understand God's plan for me.

"You are going to stop just like that?" she asked.

"Just like that," I replied.

"Well, you will have to do that because I don't allow that in my homes," she stated emphatically.

When the dirt was moved, and the shrubs were planted, she paid me $50 cash. Then she told me she wanted to take me out for a meal at a Coney Island near her group home. I knew that this would be the equivalent of a formal interview. In my mind, it registered that I had to start answering questions like an educated man, instead of a street person. When I started to live on the street, I had actually altered my speech patterns, just so I wouldn't have to answer too many questions. I was subscribing to the age-old theory of "when in Rome, do as the Romans do." My speech on the streets was more vulgar, more basic and more slang-filled. When I sat down with Sheryl Carson, I made a mental note to sound more educated.

Today I couldn't tell you what I said in that interview, but I must have passed because when we were finished Miss Carson said I had the job. However, it wouldn't start right away. In the interim she would make me a group home supervisor, although I would have to be trained in dispensing medicine and learning emergency techniques, such as a cardio pulmonary resuscitation (CPR). I agreed. She told me she could give me a place to live in the home, starting that evening.

"Does it have utilities?" I asked.

She laughed. "Of course it does."

"How about a shower?"

She continued laughing. "Yes, it does."

"And I can have anything I want to eat?"

"Absolutely."

The last thing she told me is that she knew who I had been hanging out with, and she wasn't going to allow those people in her house. "Don't you be bringing them there," she said.

I promised her I wouldn't. Miss Carson let me off, outside my area, so I could walk to the abandoned house to get my few remaining possessions. She said she would call her employee, Bill Scott, and tell him I was coming that day. I would go on the payroll on Monday. But God wasn't through sending me His message.

When I left Miss Carson's vehicle, despite what I said, I wasn't ready to come clean. I took my $65 and headed straight to the liquor store. I bought a pint of Mohawk, a 40-ounce cold Black Label, and headed toward a dope house for the purchase of some drugs. I kept reminding myself, what I had heard, and that I committed to a new job. I still made the purchase. You can rationalize anything when you're an addict. I told myself this would be my last drink and then I was going to buy my last drugs. Then I was going to Miss Carson's place.

However, it didn't work out that way. When I took a swig of the Mohawk Vodka, I didn't feel anything. There was no burn, no rush. It was wet, but it was like water. I started to curse. I immediately believed that the store owners sold me some bogus liquor. I surmised that they had filled the bottle with water to make extra profit. I just threw the bottle on the ground.

Then I ran into another addict and I told him I was on my way to buy my last drugs. Of course, he wanted to go with me.

On the way, I opened the beer and there was no beer taste. Water again. I was cursing again. I had spent my hard-earned money, and now I had been ripped off by a greedy store owner. I couldn't even get high.

I gave the guy my beer, he drank it and said: "There ain't nothing wrong with this beer." He polished it off.

By now, we were at the dope house, and I purchased drugs. But when I lit up, there was nothing. Then I realized what was happening. I realized that God had a plan. I gave the rest of the dope to my acquaintance and started to walk away. "I'm done with drugs," I announced. There were others in this dope house, regulars who knew me well, they were all muttering as I left. "That man has gone crazy."

The other thing I remember is that when I went to reclaim my belongings at the vacant house, the door fell off the hinge as I was walking out. How about that for symbolism? God was adding some theatrics to his miracle on August 17.

When I arrived at Miss Carson's group home, everything I owned was in a garbage bag. I was wearing a full beard—I hadn't shaved in a long, long time—when I met Bill Scott for the first time. He was clearly skeptical when I came into the house. He gave me a razor and pointed me toward where I could bathe and make myself presentable. He even cut my hair with clippers.

He kept asking me whether I was sure I could do this. I knew he believed Miss Carson had made a poor decision.

"I'll be watching you," he warned me.

I told him that once I came into that house I wasn't going to be leaving for a while. My old life was just right around the corner, with the pimps, hookers and addicts. I wasn't going to tempt myself.

When I went to wash clothes, I discovered that I still had a hash pipe in my belongings. I was mortified. I ran and hurled it out the door. Bill came to me, concerned. "Where are you going?" he asked.

"I'm not going anywhere," I said, and that was finally the truth.

In a span of less than 12 hours, I had gone from a full-blown addict with no home, job or prospects to a man who knew in his heart he would no longer be involved with drugs or alcohol. I had a home and a job. Over the next several weeks, I had no withdrawal symptoms. I did wake up scared the next morning because I didn't know where I was. I wasn't used to being in a bed. A couple of times I dreamed I was using and I would immediately wake up. I would ask myself whether I was going to return to that life. I would remind myself that God had told me I was through with drugs—and I was.

What happened on August 17, 1997, was a true miracle.

CHAPTER 11

COMING BACK TO LIFE

WHEN A PERSON IS IN THE GRASP of a drug and alcohol addiction, he or she is not even living in the neighborhood of reality. The addict's mind is imprisoned and he or she isn't even given an hour a day to exercise intellectual capacity. The information super highway doesn't often reach crack houses, street corners and vacant buildings. During my lost days on the streets of Detroit, if life had been discovered on another planet, I might not have known about it until aliens were parading down Jefferson Avenue. When I was standing on the corners with the whores, pimps and addicts, we weren't talking about the liberation of Palestine or whether the Democrats would ever regain control of the house. We were just "talking shit" as they would say in the hood. If we weren't cursing at, or running away from the police, then we were scheming about ways to earn enough money to buy our next fifth of Mohawk Vodka.

Occasionally, I would catch a glimpse of a television report while I was buying my liquor in the local stores. I had no idea what was happening in sports, the country or the world. The boundaries of my life were the streets and vacant homes around Lakewood and Jefferson. Most importantly, I had no idea what was happening with my friends and family. When I became married to drugs and alcohol, life moved on without me. My children grew up in my absence. Buddies married. Friends had children. Relatives died. When you begin to wage war against your drug addiction, it is like emerging from a coma. You become shocked by the events that have transpired while you were in love with alcohol and a crack pipe.

When the voice brought me back to reality on August 17, 1997, it really was like I had been awakened from a 15-year slumber. I had some contact with my ex-wife and children during that period, but there was virtually no contact with them over my final two years living on the streets. My family was living just a few miles away from the vacant house where I spent many nights. But truthfully I was a million miles away because of my addiction. From the early 1980s until 1997, there was almost no contact with my friends and extended family members. The addiction is a powerful force, but the embarrassment factor was also significant. What I wanted most in my life was to earn the respect of those around me. I didn't want anyone to see me as the street person I had become.

Many addicts steal from their family to support their habit or borrow excessive amounts of money. I never did that, even in my drug and alcohol-altered state, I had pride. I refused to drag my family into my lowlife existence. In the earlier years of my addiction, I did occasionally phone members of my family. I told white lies about where I was living and how I was doing. To hear me talk to my family members on the telephone in those days, you would have thought that prosperity was just around the corner for me. I probably didn't fool anyone. Word had spread among my family that Billy Taylor was living like a bum. To be honest, in my final homeless years, no one in my family could even be confident I was still among the living.

When I finally got back up in 1997, I had relationships to renovate and rebuild. You can't quit drinking and abusing drugs on August 17 and expect that your life will be restored and everyone is going to forgive you by the following afternoon. It takes time to clear your mind and prepare yourself for what lies ahead. I didn't even

As a college football superstar, B. T. tasted the nectar of fame. In ensuing years, he would slip into the depths of despair, and then *Get Back Up*, as Dr. Billy Taylor.

As an inmate at Milan Prison, Billy Taylor would hone his skills as a talented poet to cope with the extreme adversity of living while incarcerated.

Friend and Academic advisor Dr. Paul E. Meacham. Dr. Taylor refers to him as "the Bo Schembechler of my academic career."

Dr. Carol Harter presents Dr. Taylor with his Doctorate degree at UNLV. Taylor is living proof you can "Get Back Up!"

Professor Billy Taylor providing tutelage and mentoring to students at the Community College of Southern Nevada. (fall 2003).

Teaching a 1st grade class at Mountain-view Christian School in Las Vegas. This was the first job in Billy Taylor's new career.

Dr. Billy Taylor and his former teammates gather in Ann Arbor for an historic reunion.

Former teammate and celebrated sports anchor, Jim Brandstatter and Dr. Taylor reflect during U. of M.'s 125 year reunion.

Friend and former Michigan team surgeon the late Dr. Gerald O'Connor performed Dr. Taylor's first knee surgery at the end of his junior season at Michigan.

Billy Taylor with friend and teammate Fri Seyferth, in Calgary, Alberta, Canada in the Fall of 1973. Both lined up again in the same backfield with the Calgary Stampeders of the Canadian Football League.

November 20, 1971. "Touchdown Billy Taylor" scored the winning touchdown to beat Ohio State 10-7, and secure U of M's first undefeated regular season since 1947. B.T., #94 Butch Carpenter and #74 Tony Smith are jubilant. Also, #42 broke the legendary Tom Harmon's all-time record for career rushing touchdowns.

With former teammates and friends Tom Neiman and Chuck DeKeado, along with old friend Tom Wiesner, formerly of the University of Wisconsin Badgers at the Big Dogs restaurant in Las Vegas.

30th Anniversary class of 1969. The team is considered one of
the best Wolverine squads of all time.

Good friend and Dr. Billy Taylor's #1
fan, Gordon York of Pontiac, Michigan.

Former Teammates: Pete Newell, Mike
Smith, Don Moorehead, former U of M
coach Chuck Stobart (now at Ohio State),
Glen Doughty, and Dick Caldarazzo.

Flanked by Detroit television anchor,
Robbie Timmons, and Cheryl Elliott
at B.T.'s U of M Football team 30 year
reunion in Ann Arbor.

Dr. Billy Taylor with his coach Bo
Schembechler and Bo's dynamic wife
Kathy.

Son William Taylor III and friend
Anthony Carter (former Michigan All-
American and NFL Star).

Friends, teammates and roommates "The
Mellow Men": Glen Doughty, Mike
Taylor, Mike Oldham and Dr. Taylor.

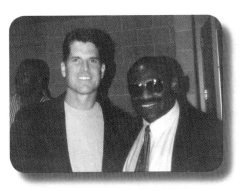

Friend, former U of M and NFL
quarterback, Jim Harbaugh.

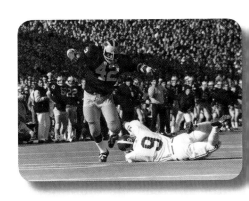

Billy Taylor eludes Spartan tackler and goes in for a touchdown.
U of M 34- MSU 20.

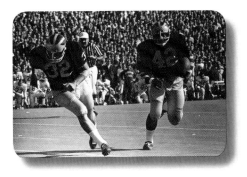

Billy Taylor goes around the left side for
a second touchdown against Michigan
State University. Seyferth leads the way.
October 17, 1970.

Brian Healey and son at 125 year reunion.

Friend, Dan Diedorf, All-American, All-Pro and Pro Football Hall of Famer. Dierdorf said Billy Taylor carried their team.

Congressman John Conyers of Michigan has established an enduring legacy in his unprecedented career.

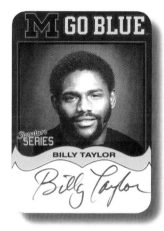

"Touchdown Billy Taylor" immortalized in the popular trading card set produced by TK Legacy.

October 30, 1971: Billy Taylor breaks away for a touchdown against Indiana. (Photo courtesy of The Bentley Historical Library, University of Michigan.)

Teammates Fritz Seyferth, Guy Murdoch, Frank Gusich, and Dana Coin.

Dr. Taylor smiles when spotting former teammate Dave Brown at a U of M reunion.

125 year All- Class Reunion. Dr. Billy Taylor with Mr. and Mrs. Don Canham.

Supporting the Wolverines at Crisler Arena in 2003. Earlier, Dr. Taylor met with friend and basketball Coach Tommy Amaker.

Friends and former teammates, quarterback Kevin Casey and defensive back Don Eaton.

Friend and former team trainer Lindsay McClain. Lindsay retired as the head trainer of the San Francisco 49ers.

Former teammates John Gabler and Jim Mandich.

Dr. Taylor considers his former Defensive Coach Jim Young a football genius.

Dr. Billy Taylor tells his son William III that Don Canham helped revolutionize college football with his marketing prowess.

All-American football star Bob Chappius and Bump Elliott, former Michigan Head Coach and Athletic Director.

Friends and former University of Michigan Athletic Directors Don Canham and Tom Goss.

Michigan vs. Ohio State, 100th meeting, 2003. Fritz Seyferth, Mike Taylor, and Dana Coin.

Dr. Billy Taylor enjoying the hospitality of the U of M Alumni Association while visiting the association's President and CEO Steve Grafton.

Proudly wearing his "Bo's Boys" t-shirt.

Dr. Billy Taylor and Coach Bo Schembechler, an icon in University of Michigan athletic history, has been like a second father to Taylor.

Former teammate Jim "The Rope" Betts.

125th All-Class Reunion, L-R Dave Brown, Billy Taylor, Bo Schembechler (B.T.'s surrogate father) and Carl Russ.

Dr. Billy Taylor congratulates his friend, Tim Chambers, after Coach Chambers guided the CCSN baseball team to the National Junior College Athletic Association World Series Championship.

Former Michigan Head Coach Gary Moeller at the 125th year U of M All-Class Reunion. While he was an assistant coach during Billy Taylor's playing days, he helped instill in B.T to never give up and "Get Back Up."

Dr. Billy Taylor reliving some of his glorious days at "The Big House" where he established his legendary status as one of the greatest Wolverines of all-time.

Enjoying the pre-game ambience and signing autographs for fans with roommate and teammate Glen Doughty.

Nevada Congresswoman Shelly Berkley.

Friend and classmate Dr. Tom Peacock, Associate Vice President of Human Resources at Community College Southern Nevada.

Dr. Dale Anderson, Professor at University of Nevada, Las Vegas. He is a good friend of Dr. Billy Taylor and he also served on Taylor's Doctoral committee.

Dr. Billy Taylor arrives at his first Las Vegas home, 2001. It is an incredible journey from living on the streets of Detroit.

Dr. Taylor expressing extreme joy and satisfaction after graduating from the University of Las Vegas at Thomas & Mack Arena. He got back up and achieved his goal, earning his Doctoral Degree in the program of Education Leadership! With an indomitable will, the power of God, and the help of others, Dr. Billy Taylor achieved a goal that many believed to be impossible.

With the help of Fritz Seyferth's block, Billy Taylor scores against Virginia, September 19, 1971. Final Score 56-0, University of Michigan.

B.T. performs the famous Billy Taylor shuffle after scoring another one of his record setting touchdowns.

"Touchdown Billy Taylor" kept legendary announcer Bob Ufer enthusiastically busy when Ufer described some of B.T.'s extraordinary exploits.

With B.T. anchoring the running game, the Wolverines posted a sterling record of 26-4 in the contests that Billy Taylor played in. Had Taylor played in all four seasons for the Michigan football squad, he may have set additional records that would be all-time marks today.

When B.T. hit the open field, few defenders ever caught the fleet footed powerhouse. (Photo courtesy of The Bentley Historical Library, University of Michigan)

Billy Taylor still holds the all time U of M record of 102.4 average rushing yards per game.

B.T.'s hard driving running style and affable personality made him one of the most liked Wolverines among his teammates. (Photo courtesy of The Bentley Historical Library, University of Michigan)

Billy Taylor, 1972 Rose Bowl action vs. Stanford. He retired as the teams all time leading rusher with 3,072 career yards. (Photo courtesy of The Bentley Historical Library, University of Michigan)

Number 42 earned All-American football honors in 1969,1970, and 1971. (Photo courtesy of The Bentley Historical Library, University of Michigan)

B.T. was recruited by 57 different colleges before ultimately becoming a superstar with the Wolverines. (Photo courtesy of The Bentley Historical Library, University of Michigan)

Taylor practicing some of his famous B.T. lateral slides. Today, he is still considered one of the finest ever at his postition in the history of college football. 1970. (Photo courtesy of The Bentley Historical Library, University of Michigan)

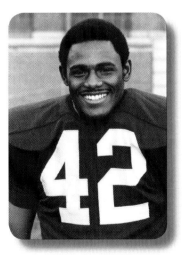

No coach, past or present, motivates the team like the legendary Bo Schembechler while driving the maize and blue to the practice field in preparation of dominating their next opponent. 1970. (Photo courtesy of The Bentley Historical Library, University of Michigan)

Billy Taylor displays pre-season excitement as he begins the 1969 campaign as a budding superstar. (Photo courtesy of The Bentley Historical Library, University of Michigan)

Bo Schembechler was not only a leader and mentor to players on the field but also off the field as well. 1970. (Photo courtesy of The Bentley Historical Library, University of Michigan)

B.T. revels in the thunderous applause of 100,000 exuberant "Big House" fans after another one of his breathtaking rushes. 1971. (Photo courtesy of The Bentley Historical Library, University of Michigan)

Randy Logan, Billy Taylor, Don Moorhead, Glenn Doughty, 1970. (Photo courtesy of The Bentley Historical Library, University of Michigan)

Billy Taylor patterned his powerful running style after the Cleveland Brown's great Jim Brown.

Touchdown Billy Taylor's final and greatest touchdown against Ohio State helping Michigan attain the number 2 ranking in the nation. Also, the victory guaranteed the Wolverines their 1st undefeated regular season since 1947.

While in Las Vegas, Immortal Investment's Publisher Mike Reddy congratulates Dr. Taylor after arranging to publish the incredible life story of B. T. Both believe the book will sell over 100,000 copies and inspire thousands of readers. Also, *Get Back Up*, is slated to be a major motion picture.

Mr. & Mrs. Hockey's Business Agent, Del Reddy, *The People's Champion,* Willie Horton and Pro-Football HOF writer Jerry Green with future College Football Hall Of Famer Dr. Taylor at the Immortal Investments Publishing book launch celebration at Comerica Park on June 21, 2005. (Photo by Lynn Gregg)

Dr. Taylor and Jennifer Hilliker, Assistant to the Publishers of Immortal Investments Publishing, show their excitement of the impending publication of *Get Back Up!* (Photo by Lynn Gregg)

Co-author of *Get Back Up* and *The Peoples Champion*, Kevin Allen shares his pride of co-writing the books of both legends, Dr. Billy Taylor and Willie Horton. (Photo by Lynn Gregg)

Immortal Investments video pro, Dave Story, discusses the incredible life story of Dr. William L. Taylor Jr. (Photo by Lynn Gregg)

Immortal Investments Publishing book formatter, Jill Thomas, is honored to provide her expertise to make *Get Back Up* number one. (Photo by Lynn Gregg)

University of Michigan Director of Development for the W.K. Kellogg Center, Douglas Bechler, speaks with Karen Sazlaw and Dr. Taylor about B.T.'s glory days at U of M. (Photo by Lynn Gregg)

Mr. & Mrs. Hockey's Business Agent Aaron Howard and Ford Motor Companies Larry Gach, both graduates of U of M, with their favorite wolverine star, #42 Billy Taylor. (Photo by Lynn Gregg)

Dr. Taylor compliments *Get Back Up* photo formattor Steve Waetjen. (Photo by Lynn Gregg)

leave the group home on Lakewood for two weeks after I began living and working there. I didn't contact my immediate family for two months because I wanted to make sure I was clean and I wanted to save some money. My job provided me with $200 per week, plus room and board. With my first check, I bought new shoes, plus some trousers and shirts, and I went to a movie for the first time in years. Then I splurged on M & Ms, nachos and cheese. I never ate treats like that during the peak of my addiction. If I had two dollars, it was going into a pint of liquor, not into a bag of candy that "melts in your mouth, not in your hand." The only food I ate in those days would have been sandwiches that someone would give me for working, or the scraps I could scrounge up at the Kentucky Fried Chicken when the unsold food was discarded.

Once my head was clear, I became worried about my health. What kind of damage had I done to my body over the years? A physical examination, done a week or two after I quit drinking, showed no liver or heart damage, usually associated with alcoholism. And though I spent considerable time on the streets I contacted no diseases connected with street life. It was remarkable considering I spent considerable time with pimps, hookers, addicts and others who don't make health issues a top priority.

My weight had dropped to 165 at its lowest point—about 40 pounds under my college playing weight. Although the drugs and alcohol were killing me slowly, sometimes I wonder if my eating regimen in those days might have been healthier than the one I have today. It was definitely low calorie, and not much fat, except on the days when the KFC employees had leftover chicken and potatoes for me. On many days, my daily food intake consisted of a couple of pieces of bread with some meat on it, or a can of sardines. Back then, I had no stomach issues.

Today, I cannot eat what I want, I'm looking to lose a few pounds, and I take prescription heartburn medicine. Funny how when I was on the street I never had any digestive problems. Today, I sit behind a desk and don't get the exercise I would like to get. In my homeless days, I would be constantly walking, looking for a way to earn a couple of bucks to buy my liquor. When I found work, it was usually manual labor. I would be mowing lawns, shoveling snow, or doing some heavy lifting.

When I was ready to re-connect with society, I started with my immediate family and worked my way back to Barberton, Ohio where I knew people were still angry and hurt over the bank robbery. Not long after, Sheryl Carson helped me reclaim my life, I made a pilgrimage back to Barberton to reunite with friends and family.

One stop I made was at the home of Bill and Pat Von Stein. They essentially made me a member of their family when I was growing up in Barberton. Bill was a school bus driver and Pat worked as a secretary for the school district in the administration office. The Von Steins were an involved couple; they cared about people in their community. They cared about me. I was black. They were white. But they treated me like a son. They lived at 189 Robinson, maybe a quarter-mile from U.L. Light Middle School. They met me after watching me play middle school football and almost instantly I began to view them like another set of parents. Usually Bill would be the bus driver that transported our middle school football team to away games. The Von Steins viewed me as a young, poor black child with plenty of ability, even beyond football, and they seemed to want to do whatever they could to help me realize my dreams.

I slept there as often as I liked. The Von Steins were Italian and they filled me up on spaghetti or other pasta dishes all the time. Their children, Kathy and Bill Jr., were like a younger sister and brother to me. They followed my football career from high school to college, sometimes driving to Ann Arbor even for the games. Pat even made a scrapbook for me that included newspaper clippings from my high school and college career.

One winter she knitted maize and blue ponchos and tams for all of the Mellow Men. There's a photo in this book showing us wearing them.

The Von Steins doted on me as if I carried their own bloodline. When I would visit Barberton, I would often stop at their home before going to my mother's house. Before I returned to Ann Arbor, Pop, as I called Bill Sr., would insist on taking me down to his favorite watering hole, the Sun Inn, on Tuscarawas Avenue and we would eat hamburgers and drink well into the evening.

"Hey, you guys know my son Billy Taylor," Pop would say loud enough for everyone to hear.

Everyone would laugh because they all knew me, and they all understood the close relationship I had with the Von Steins. The Von Steins were extremely proud of my success at Michigan. I think Pop liked to brag about me a little bit. It made Pop proud to bring me to his bar so we could all talk Michigan vs. Ohio State football.

Undoubtedly, it crushed them when I was arrested in Barberton for involvement in the bank robbery in 1975. They were among the first on the scene to lend their support. I didn't see them for many years as I sunk deep into the morass of depression and drugs. I wanted to see them to show them that there was a reason again to be proud of me. I had been knocked down, but I had gotten back up, just like I had on the Barberton football field.

Early in 1998, I drove into their driveway like I had a hundred times before. I ran up the front porch stairs, eager to see the look on the faces of Mom and Pop Von Stein. Their young grandchildren came to the door instead.

"Where is mom?" I asked Pat's grandkids.

They looked at me strangely. Then Bill Jr. came to the door and a look of recognition spread across his face. "BT is that you?" he asked, a smile rising on his face.

When I asked again where his parents were, his smile evaporated.

"You really don't know do you," he said, somberly. "Mom and Dad died two years ago."

His words were an emotional dagger that pierced my heart with the same excruciating pain that I felt when Bo Schembechler informed me that my mother had died, and that my Uncle Eugene and

Aunt Hattie were gone. The pain drove me to my knees and I could not stop sobbing. Tears covered my face, but they could not wash away the pain in my soul.

Bill Jr. put his arm around my shoulders and said, "BT, mom was always talking about you and wondering where you were and what you were doing. We didn't know how to reach you when they died."

He told me that Pat had died of a heart attack and Bill Sr. had succumbed to a stroke a month later. The fact that they died a month apart made sense to me because those two loved each other so deeply that it seemed impossible to fathom that one could exist without the other. It was more shocking that Pat had died first because Bill didn't take care of himself very well. He was a drinker and smoker and always said that he was going to go first. The stroke may have been the official cause of death, but I'm sure it was brought on, or at least complicated, by a broken heart.

While I was investing in a drug addiction, my brother-in-law Monroe Lewis also died, as did Orris Thomas who was married to my cousin. I didn't learn of their deaths until years after they happened. As euphoric as you feel when you become clean and sober, there is considerable grieving that must be done after you come back to life. You haven't just lost time; you have lost people and relationships. People had moved on in my absence, and some of them weren't coming back to me.

One event that happened during my drug years haunts me still to this day. When my son, Alden, was 14, he was struck in the groin by a baseball.   One of his testicles was severely damaged, but Alden didn't reveal to his mother that he was in intense pain. No 14-year-old is going to drop his slacks and show that physical problem to his mother.

When I heard about this injury a couple of years later he reminded me that I hadn't even called him on Christmas a few months before. He said he wanted to call me about the injury, but he had no idea where to begin to look. Even his mother had no idea where I could be located. "We didn't even know if you were alive or dead," Alden said later.

When the pain became excruciating, Alden showed his groin to his brother, William Lewis III, who was 16 months older. By then, the injured testicle had swollen to the size of a softball. Mortified by the sight, William made his brother seek medical attention immediately. But by then the damage was severe enough that surgery was required.

That story still haunts me to this day. My son needed his father and I wasn't there because of the romance I had with drugs and alcohol. I probably was hanging out on a street corner smoking dope the day that happened, oblivious to the pain my child was feeling.

I waited two months to call my ex-wife because I wanted to make sure the fabric of my life was sewn back together when my children saw me again. I wanted to make sure I had an address to call my own, and cash in my pocket. I wanted them to view me as a highly educated man with a meaningful job. My older boys knew I had been living on the streets, and I wanted to make sure I looked healthy when they saw me. I wanted to put on a few pounds before I met them, and I made sure I was well groomed when I saw my children again. When Sheryl Carson saw me after I got ready for my kids, she laughed. "Bill you clean up pretty good."

I couldn't be sure how my children would react to me. Would they just see the man who abandoned them in the midst of his addiction? Or would they view me as the man who loved them dearly before the lure of drugs enslaved me? Would there be anger or resentment?

My concerns were erased the minute the kids arrived at the group home. I could see in the faces of my boys that they were just relieved that I didn't look emaciated or near death. They seemed almost surprised that I didn't look like a wino, with a scraggly beard and a weathered face. My five-year-old daughter, Mariah, named after my mother, bounded out of the car in full stride, yelling: "Daddy, Daddy, Daddy." I couldn't believe how much she had changed, how much older she looked. She didn't look bitter or angry. She looked thrilled to see me, like someone who had deeply missed her father.

Mariah cried for several minutes, but her father cried even longer.

Obviously, I wasn't able to completely re-connect with my children in the first meeting. It takes time to rebuild trust and to re-establish a parent-child relationship that has been non-existent for more than two years. As someone who fully understands the horror of drug abuse, you worry about your own children falling prey to the evils of intoxicants. You wonder whether your illness will be passed along to them. Medical research has demonstrated that alcoholism, for example, does run in certain families. You can't bear that thought. You pray that your children won't find themselves on the path to destruction that you were on.

A year after I walked away from my life of drugs, an incident brought me to a confrontation with one of my greatest fears in life.

I was playing on the front grass with six-year-old Mariah in the front yard. She was laughing, giggling, jumping around like it was the first day of summer vacation.

"Daddy, I use drugs,' she said, her energy still bubbling over. My sharp stare caused her to freeze in her steps. "What did you say?" I said, way too harshly. Mariah began to cry, tears cascading down her cheeks. She was visibly afraid. She was trembling. I picked her up and held her in the air to allow us to be face-to-face. "Don't ever say that again," I said. "Don't ever let me hear you say that again—do you hear me?" Still crying, Mariah says, "I'm sorry Daddy. I was only playing."

"Don't ever play like that again—do you understand?" I repeated. "Yes Daddy," she said, still petrified.

My ex-wife witnessed the incident and she tried to reduce the tension. "Bill," she offered, "Mariah was only playing and she doesn't even know what she was saying."

"I know," I said. "That's why I don't ever want to hear her say that again."

By then I realized I needed to go into the house to calm down. Mariah's innocent words had brought me to a place where I didn't want to be. It doesn't scare me to think about where I've been. It scares me to think about someone I love might go there in the future.

CHAPTER 12

DR. WILLIAM TAYLOR IS BORN

WHO WOULD HAVE BELIEVED THAT MY road to recovery from alcohol and drug addiction would lead to Sin City. It's rather ironic that it was in Las Vegas where I would be reunited with my dreams and ambition. In a city where lying, bluffing, drinking and sinning are a way of life, I found stability, peace and truth.

When I try to explain to everyone how I know that God has been involved in my recovery, I point to my place of residence. "During my addiction days, if I lived in a city where free drinks were available I would be dead by now."

After a year of employment by Sheryl Carson at Family Tyes, I had commenced to think about pursuing my dreams again. I thought about continuing my education—perhaps to honor the memory of my mother who always wanted me to be Dr. William Taylor because she liked the sound of Dr. Martin Luther King. Primarily, I just wanted to prove to myself that I could reach that level of accomplishment.

Sheryl Carson had taken her employees on a trip to Las Vegas in June 1998. While I was there, I read in an article in the Las Vegas *Review Journal* newspaper about how the Clark County School District had grown by about 9,000 students over one year. It was the fastest growing school district in the country. That seemed completely unbelievable to me, because, in Detroit, schools were being closed because of a lack of enrollment. To me, it seemed like another sign from the Almighty. Then I read another article that mentioned that the local Community College of Southern Nevada, where I now work, had 25,000 students. (Now it has 36,000 students). That just overwhelmed me. Then the article said that there was a shortage of teachers and administrators in the area and I knew that a move to Las Vegas was part of the plan. I felt as if my master's degree would get me a job at the community college.

Room and board had been part of wages at Family Tyes, which allowed me to give some money to my ex-wife and to save some too. I tried to reconcile my marriage, but my wife had no trust in my rehabilitation. She assumed that my recovery was another lie, and that I would eventually crumble and return to the streets. How could she be blamed for thinking that, given my history? I realized that all signs were pointing me toward a change of address.

I had a friendship with the sister-in-law of a former Michigan football player, and she encouraged me to come out there and live with her until I found a job. At first, I was just going out there while I interviewed but then I decided that it would be better if I just committed. Sheryl Carson was disappointed, but I told her, "It's just something I have to do." She supported me.

I packed up my 1988 Pontiac Bonneville—I called it Black Beauty—and headed to Las Vegas with $1,800 in my pocket and dreams in my heart. Sheryl bought that car for me, and said she would take the money out of my check. She took a little bit, but she never took the entire amount. The car was really a gift to me. I appreciated that car.

Within two weeks, I had a job as substitute teacher for $50 per day in a Christian school. I was only working a couple of days per week. It was difficult to get into the Clark County system because I had a felony conviction on my record and that eliminated me from consideration. I knew that the public school system did more extensive background checks. I decided to lie and take my chances.

When I was asked if I had ever been convicted of a felony, I checked "No."

I worked for about six weeks before the background check uncovered my criminal record. I was immediately fired. That depressed me.

To make matters worse, my living situation with my friend had become intolerable. Her sons were drinking and partying and I wanted to move out in the worse way. I had spent all of my savings. All I had left was a check for $120 from the Christian Academy. However, I saw an apartment ad in the newspaper for a move-in special for $99. I took it without knowing where I was going to get next month's rent. I moved into the place on Christmas Eve.

My friend said, "Stay one more day—we are having a party."

"Nope," I said, "I'm going now." I just knew that it was time to go. I slept on the floor that night because I had no furniture. I was happy as a boy on Christmas morning because I had my own place. Then events started to happen. I got a job as an adjunct teacher, and no one asked me the question about a felony. I felt blessed.

After working as an instructor at the community college for a couple of years, I began to believe it was time to pursue my doctorate at the University of Nevada-Las Vegas. I asked Dr. Paul Meacham to be my advisor. He was like the Bo Schembechler of doctorate advisors.

"Don't be fooling around," he would say. "I'm not going to be around forever. I'm going to be retiring soon. And don't waste my time by being ABD." I told him I did not even know what that was, and he said it was an acronym for All-But Dissertation. Some students complete the course work for their doctorate, but can't, won't, or don't, complete their dissertation. "Don't be an ABD on me," he said.

I promised him that wasn't my intention. He told me he would stay active until I finished and he did exactly that.

I had concerns about my own preparedness. Had I been doing this in the late 1970s, I would have been full of confidence. Not only had I been absent from the world of academia, I had essentially dropped out of the life. I passed my Graduate Records Exam, but with a low range score. When I showed up to take the writing test, I had to walk out of the room and inform Dr. Meacham that I had to re-schedule the test. I wasn't ready. I returned home and formulated ideas about what might be on the test, and practiced my writing abilities. I worked night and day for two weeks to sharpen my rusty skills. I needed the work because I hadn't exactly been crafting educational theories while I was living on the streets. When I took the test, I passed it.

When I started the pursuit of my doctorate in 1999, there were about 15 people in my group, and most of them were quite scholarly. There was also a black woman in the group named Marsha Robinson. In the first class, I think we both believed we were just a little over our heads because in that first class, we were assigned a 10-page paper and eight chapters of reading before the next class. At the class intermission, Miss Robinson said to me, "This is going to be a lot of work. I hope we make it."

"I'm just going to keep on coming," I said. "I'm just going to keep on coming." That is something Dr. Charles Moody taught me at Michigan. You must be relentless in your pursuit of a doctorate. You have to keep on coming, and if you get knocked down you have to get back up. I had the same mentality I had as a football player. Before my last carry against Ohio State, I told myself, *I am not going down.* When I started my doctorate, I told myself, *I am not going to fail.*

I was correct in anticipating that my street years would cost me. I simply wasn't current on the phrasing and terminology of higher education today. Remember, I was only clean and sober for just over a year when I decided to pursue my doctorate. While most of the people in my group were working the field, I was drinking Black Labels on Jefferson and Lakewood. I had to look up every concept and theory. I had to read other material just to understand what I was reading for my class assignment. It was almost like I was doing double the work. I stayed up countless hours making up for those lost years in the drug world. The extra work paid off and I completed all of my classes with a 3.92 grade-point average. It was time for my dissertation.

Dr. Meacham prepared me for the dissertation like Bo prepared us for the Rose Bowl. He made sure I was ready. He was old school, and he wouldn't let me get by with average. I went to see him every week for a year.

He was honest. He told me, "Bill, you aren't writing at the doctoral level."

Just like Bo wouldn't let me just be a good back, Dr. Meacham wouldn't just let me be a mediocre student. He forced me to re-write passages several times. I must have read about 100 books to complete my research. This was much more difficult to complete than my course work. Every comma must be right. Every source must be documented. Every footnote must be properly placed. I wasn't ready for this challenge when I started, but I persevered.

The title of my dissertation was "Identifying the Barriers to Access to Higher Education for African-America Students: Opinions of Successful African-American Educators."

In my acknowledgments, I said I dedicated my work to my children because I wanted "to provide an example for them." Given that they knew my history, this was very important to me. I also mentioned the guidance that my mother Mariah Marie Taylor had provided me. It was also being done in my father's memory, and I thanked Sheryl Carson for her kindness.

In my opening, I wrote: "Educational discrimination against African-Americans within the United States has been an unfortunate fact of life since our nation's beginning. Within the U.S. Constitution itself, Negroes (as African-Americans were then called) are explicitly referred to as unequal. As Article 1, Section 2 of the United States Constitution states, Representatives...shall be apportioned among the several States...according to their respective Numbers, *which shall be determined by adding to the whole number of free persons and three-fifths of all other persons [italics added]* ("Constitution", 2000, pp. 26-27"). The 14th amendment (1868) abolished this rule."

It's clear from that opening where I would be heading with this research. My conclusion was that the playing field is not level and there is work that needs to be done to assure that blacks have equal access to higher education.

When the writing was completed to Dr. Meacham's satisfaction, I owned 150 polished pages. That was the easiest aspect of the process.

Dr. Meacham explained the next phase this way: "The only two times when you are truly alone is when you are born and when you defend your dissertation."

It was one of the most psychologically draining experiences of my life. It is essentially an educational gauntlet. You meet with a panel to discuss your work, and it's like being in front of a panel of federal judges. They pick apart your argument, idea by idea, sentence by sentence, comma by comma. They challenge you on your conclusion. Really, it's combat of the mind. Most defenses of dissertations last 45 minutes to an hour. I'm told. My defense lasted one hour and 45 minutes. It seemed like 8 or 10 hours. It was an intimidating process.

During my defense, Dr. Gerald Kops was my chief antagonist on my four-person panel. He played the Devil's Advocate. He attacked and probed my work, probably to make me stronger. However, it didn't make it any less painful. My research was sound. I had sent out questionnaires to more than 100 successful black Americans, primarily in the field of education. I received a 30-45 percent response, which was high. I asked these people to cite the greatest academic barriers facing African Americans today, and in almost every response, there was a mention of finances and discrimination.

I vividly recall Dr. Kops asking me this question, "Bill, how can you say that there is discrimination and inequity for Blacks as it pertains to equal access to higher education when W.E.B. Dubois was the first African-American to receive a doctorate degree from Harvard back in the 1890's?" As shocking as it was for me to hear such a question being raised by any current higher education faculty member, I must say that it was consistent with past challenges presented by Dr. Kops. I remember how quiet the room became right after Dr. Kop's question; I took a quiet deep breath before answering because the question had accomplished its purpose, to shock and irritate me. I wanted to ask him why would he ask me such an asinine question but I knew not to answer a question with a question. Out of the corner of my eye, I noticed Dr. Meacham sitting to my immediate right, rear back in his chair, I knew what that meant.

Every eye in the room rested upon me as I began to make my calculated response. I said, "Dr. Kops, perhaps it is not a well-known fact but Dr. W.E.B. Dubois came to Harvard with an earned bachelors degree from Fisk College (now University) and it was not accepted. He was reclassified as a junior at Harvard. Subsequently, he completed his bachelors (a second time) at Harvard. He persisted and earned his masters in 1891 and doctorate degree at Harvard in 1895. And, later he was quoted as saying, "I was in Harvard but not of it." I saw subtle smiles from Dr. Anderson, Dr. Troutman and I heard a very pleased Dr. Meacham laugh out loud and say, "Gerry (Dr. Gerald Kops), hell if Dr. W.E.B. Dubois had the opportunity to respond to Bill's questionnaire he'd probably write a book pertaining to the discrimination he faced while earning his doctorate degree at Harvard in the 1800's.

Dr. Kops is a friend today, but in that defense I had to verbally joust with him over my conclusions. He made me think that he wasn't accepting my conclusion. He challenged me, and forced me step up and respond.

Everything is formal during a defense. There is no cordiality. It's a very serious, professional atmosphere. Dr. Meacham is in there, but you are expected to answer the questions, not him.

When the defense was completed, I was asked to step out of the room while they discussed my responses. When the door closed behind me, I heard an echo and it reminded me when I reported to prison in Oxford. That sound of a closing metal door always has an impact on me. However, once in the hallway, I leaned against the wall. I was breathing heavy, and I felt exhausted. I kept reviewing my answers. *Was I thorough? Did I stay on point? Did I answer every question?* That's what I was thinking about. I was actually in the hallway 10 minutes, but it seemed like two hours. It's like waiting for a verdict.

When I returned to the room, the panel members were all standing like pallbearers at a funeral. Dr. Meacham stepped up first, and said, "Let me be the first to congratulate you, Dr. Taylor."

There were no words in my dramatically improved vocabulary to convey the joy I felt. I just grabbed each one of them, one by one, and kissed them on the cheek.

Here's another part of the story, which is also important. During the pursuit of my doctoral degree, the administrators were aware that I was a convicted felon. However, no one knew that I had been jobless, and ultimately homeless, for many years. They didn't know that I had gone through 20 years of substance abuse. I was ashamed about that part of my history. I thought it might undermine my educational pursuits. One reason why I wanted to leave Michigan is that thousands of people knew that Billy Taylor got "jammed up," as they say on the streets.

"Why didn't you tell me?" Meacham asked when he found out about my life on the street through a newspaper article.

"Would it have mattered?" I asked.

He never said whether it would have made a difference, and I think it would not have because he was like Schembechler in that he didn't bend any rules. Both men just inspire to succeed by working with the existing rules.

Actually, I didn't plan it that way, but it was better that it worked out that way. I needed to accomplish this without any special consideration. Dr. Meacham did admit to me after I earned my Ed.D that some people didn't want me admitted to the program because of my criminal record.

Tears rolled down my face when I walked across the stage to receive my doctorate degree at the Thomas & Mack Arena. My feet never touched the stage. I floated across the stage. The only basis for comparison I have is the winning touchdown run I had against Ohio State in 1971. That was my greatest moment in athletics. This was my greatest moment in my personal life. I thought about my late mother as I walked across that stage. I thought about how proud she would have been to have witnessed this event. Dr. William Taylor. She would have liked the sound of that.

Every black family in American probably had a picture of Dr. King somewhere in the house. We had a black and white television in our house, and my mother always became more interested if a black man was on the screen. She would turn up the volume if Sidney Portier or Sammy Davis Jr. or Harry Belafonte appeared in front of her. However, mother would want the house hushed if Dr. King was speaking on TV. "Be quiet," she would say sternly. "Listen to what Dr. King is saying."

I listened to Dr. King talk about his dreams of racial equality. I was mesmerized by the eloquence of his voice. The power of his words overwhelmed me. His wisdom inspired me. As he was carrying the flag for the Civil Rights Movement in the 1960s, I was dreaming about following in his footsteps by earning a doctorate degree.

When that was achieved. I was proud to be Dr. William Taylor, I was also proud that my dissertation was about a subject that obviously Dr. King would have appreciated.

Of the 15 in my group that started in pursuit of the doctorate degree, I recall that only about 10 achieved it by 2003. One of them was Marsha Robinson. She tapped me on the shoulder and when I turned around, she was nose-to-nose with me.

"Brother, I kept coming," she said.

"Yes, you did," I answered.

We both laughed a victor's laugh, full of pride and vigor.

However, the presentation of my diploma was not my most emotional moment. That had come a few days earlier, at the campus bookstore, after I purchased my cap and gown.

When I looked for a gown, shroud and cap worn by the doctoral recipient, I simply couldn't find them. When I went to the counter for help, an employee brought me back to the section of regular caps and gowns. "No, I'm receiving a doctorate degree."

"Oh," she said, maybe showing just a bit of surprise. "What's your doctorate in?"

"Educational Leadership," I said.

"Congratulations," she said.

She pointed me to the doctoral collection. I picked and brought it to the cashier who asked whether I wanted to buy or rent. "I definitely want to buy this," I said.

I was still in command of my emotions until I began to walk out the door with the gown in a bag. I started to cry uncontrollably. I was sobbing loudly, tears pouring down my cheeks. It was as if someone had poured a cup of water on my face. I would turn my head away from people entering the store. But it was obvious to everyone that I was bawling. Everyone was looking at me, probably wondering what could cause such pain in my life. When I returned to my car, I still couldn't bring a halt to the tears.

I called Sheryl Carson's mother, Marie Polk, and told her what happened. "Son, those are tears of joy," she said. "Those are tears of joy. It's all over. You've done it. Congratulations Dr. Taylor."

EPILOGUE

WITH ALL THAT HAS HAPPENED IN MY life, I don't believe in coincidence. I believe in God. To me it's the only explanation for how I was transformed from a homeless, hard-core drug and alcohol addict to a responsible citizen in the time it takes to say "William Taylor come forth."

In the eight years since my miracle, I've never had a relapse, never even had a close call. After I downed my last drink, I didn't get blackouts. I didn't cramp. I didn't get sick. God spared me from the pain of withdrawal.

People ask me if I've sought any psychological counseling, attended Alcoholic Anonymous meetings or talked to a professional about my rehabilitation. My response is "Why should I do that? I have the universe's best counselor—our Lord and Savior."

I'm sure some people don't believe me, but I know what I heard that day and I know that before that day I had failed miserably when I tried earthly remedies to defeat my illness. Divine intervention was my only answer. Was it an angel, or God himself? I can't answer that. But I know exactly what I heard.

I also don't believe it's a coincidence that my favorite book was *Theophilus North*, Thornton Wilder's last major work. In that book, set in Newport, Rhode Island, a teacher explores life while involving himself in a variety of different professions beyond his own.

Although I would replay different acts of life over, if given the chance, I also know that like Theophilis North, I've learned much about myself through the chapters in my life. I've been a football player, a celebrity, teacher, convict, father, principal, an Alaskan laborer, a homeless man, a college instructor and a man addressed as Dr. Taylor.

I think that book is my favorite so that I would know that I could learn from all of the experiences that I've had.

Today, I still work for the Community College of Southern Nevada and I have formed Billy Taylor Initiatives, BTI, (Billytaylorinitiatives.com) a private service organization that works with the players, coaches, athletic directors and administrators to identify the positive and negative manifestations of transitional dynamics. BTI has developed an understanding of fundamental causes, predictable attitudes and priority issues affecting an athletic program and follows up with recommendations and activities to achieve both institutional and individual success. Two quotes come to mind as I go public with my philosophy of life. The first was written by the English Novelist, Essayist and Moral Philosopher, Aldous Huxley who said: "Experience is not what happens to you, it is what you do with what happens to you."

The second quotation was passed from my grandmother to my mother and then to me: "Sometimes the longest way around is the shortest way home."

At 56, I am approaching middle age. I say that because I plan to live to 116 years of age. I hope that the first half of my life will serve me well in the second. At this stage, I have developed a critical core of beliefs and values that will sustain me through the next 60 to 70 years:

A meaningful life must include close caring relationships, personal freedom and individual rights, optimism, behavioral self-control, self-acceptance and an unwavering faith in God.

I realize that all changes in my life must be made by me and the only person that I can change is me.

As a self-directed person, I make the choices about my life, think for myself, do good deeds, and serve God. He is where my strength comes from.

I choose to be a good friend, a trusted helper, and an effective worker. In addition, I choose to be a giving, responsible, tolerant and self-disciplined person who takes pride in daily deeds and future plans.

The most important guiding moral principle in my life is that the awesome power of the Lord is protective, loving, comforting, uplifting and most of all forgiving and redeeming! My faith in God is my source of strength and "He" influences my life everyday. With Him I am able to think clearly, experience contentment, weather storms, offer gratitude and find peace, without the use of any drugs, alcoholic beverages, cigarettes or any other mind or mood altering substance. I will continue to have inspiring dreams and shoot for the stars. I shall never retire, only change the work that I do. At the same time, I will accept the inevitable occasional disappointments that life throws my way. I now realize that every experience, even failure, has a lesson. To paraphrase Aldous Huxley, "It is what I do with those lessons that will continue to direct my life course."

I have reconnected with my family and I owe them a lot. My family truly lives up to the old African saying, "It takes a village to raise a child."

Hillary Clinton popularized it, but many Black families from slavery times through today live by that code—many don't know any other way, many don't have a choice. This was very true in my family.

My oldest sister Clara Bingham, 76, now lives in Akron, Ohio, with my cousin Willie Bee Bibbs on Owens Street.

All of my oldest sisters are old enough to be my mother. They each have mothered me in one way or another over the years. Clara (76), Lucille (74), Juanita (71), and my oldest brother Felix (69), were from my mom's first marriage to Mr. Ware. Clara, Lucille and Felix were raised by our Aunt Minnie in Joiner, Arkansas, through most of their childhood.

While Juanita remained with my mom and grandmother (Georgia Wells, deceased since 1966) in neighboring Hoxie, Arkansas, which is the place that my mother returned to have me after she moved from Hoxie to Memphis, Tennessee. Clara moved to St. Louis, Missouri, at age 19. She soon married, moved to Flint, Michigan, and subsequently relocated to Barberton and Akron, Ohio, to be close to mom and the rest of the family. Clara has only one child, Lee Bingham of Joiner, Arkansas.

My mom's second marriage to Mr. Jackson produced my other two older brothers, Jim, now 66 and Thomas, who is deceased. He would be 61 if he were alive. Thomas died in May of 1998, just four months prior to me moving to Las Vegas, Nevada, in September of 1998.

Lucille and Felix continued to live in Arkansas on my Aunt Minnie's farm in the small town of Joiner, Arkansas. Lucille and her only husband, Mr. Monroe Lewis, were together for 40 years. Lucille still lives on Van Buren Avenue in Barberton, Ohio. Like my mom, Lucille had seven children: Harry Ware, Robert Lewis, Ronnie Lewis, Farley Lewis, Jerome Lewis, Glen Lewis and Darlene Lewis. My brother Felix Ware has two children: Randy Ware and Barbara Ware of San Diego, California.

My youngest sister Juanita lived with mother as I did. Ironically, we both lived for long periods with my aging grandmother (Georgia Wells) during her illness and her last years in Barberton, Ohio. In my sophomore year at Baberton High School, Juanita met and married Eugene Davis of Pittsburgh, Pennsylvania, and moved there to begin here family. I remember Lucille and Juanita most during my early childhood because they were around while Clara and Felix lived in the South. Juanita had three children from her marriage to Lugene Davis: Calvin Davis of Nashville, Tennessee, Reverend Clarence Davis of Colorado Springs, Colorado, and my niece (a nurse) Marie Davis of Aliquippa, Pennsylvania.

My brother James Jackson and his wife Helen have three daughters: Valerie, Erika and Vicky.

My brother Thomas had four children from two marriages: Timothy, Thomas, Rhonda and Aretha. \

My own children, as I've mentioned in previous chapters, are all doing well.

After moving to Las Vegas, I came back to Michigan on a visit and Sheryl Carson took me back to the group home where I first lived. We passed by some pimps, prostitutes and drug addicts on the street. "Isn't that the girl you used to hang out with?" Sheryl said.

It was Little Bit. She was looking bad. Her lips were purple. Her skin looked awful. She looked sickly. She was wearing a wool stocking cap.

We pulled over, and I called her. She came over and said, "Bill, is that you?—man you look good."

"That's because I take care of myself," I said. "You have to get off the streets."

Just then a pimp started coming over. I recognized him from my days on the streets. I didn't like him then, and I don't like him now.

"Is that your man now?" I asked. She said it was, and I told her to be careful. I put $20 in her hand and told her not to give it to that guy but to use it for food, not drugs. She said she would. I knew that was probably a lie. I wished her well and I sincerely meant it. I had tears in my eyes as we pulled away. That girl meant the world to me when I was on the streets. Today, I don't know if she is alive or dead.

I want to apologize again to everyone I have hurt or disappointed throughout my troubles, particularly to the people in Barberton for disgracing the city over the bank robbery. Not everyone has forgiven me for my past sins. For example, I am not in the Barberton Hall of Fame. However, last fall I was inducted in the Summit County Hall of Fame.

In my acceptance speech, I talked about how much Bo Schembechler had meant to me and I sincerely meant it. I never lose sight of Bo's contributions to the person I've become. Other than Sheryl Carson, who I now consider my sister, no one has done as much to help me in my life. Sis has been my angel on this earth.

My buddy Thom Darden always tells me that I "should go to my grave" thanking Coach Bo Schembechler.

"He saved your life," Thom says.

I agree with that assessment. Bo Schembechler is what coaching should be about. Not only did Bo teach us how to live, he looked after his players like they were his sons. He seemed to have a special relationship with me, but he looked after all of his players. When Thom was going through a very public, ugly divorce, with the press turning his life inside out, Bo called Thom out of the blue.

"Thom," he said, "what are you doing this summer?"

When Darden said he hadn't yet found a job, Bo told him to come to the Ann Arbor and help the coaching staff institute a "two deep" defensive coverage. That job helped Thom get through some tough times.

Michigan remains a huge part of my life and through the writing of this book, I have re-connected with the alumni association. I know that my ability to survive during the troubled times was aided significantly by the lessons I learned in Ann Arbor, on and off the field.

How could it be a coincidence that God would lead me on the path to recovery within a week of the 1997 Michigan football team's first practice for what would turn out to be the school's first National Championship in almost 50 years?

Through the recent years, I've been reminded about how meaningful Michigan is to me. Don Dufek, a great Michigan defensive back from the 1970s, told me that he was inspired to attend Michigan in the 1970's by watching me run out of the backfield in 1969.

When I was at the banquet for the Summit County Hall of Fame, a couple of former Michigan players that I didn't even know were in the crowd. They were chanting, "Legend, Legend, Legend," as I walked up the microphone to make my speech.

In accepting that award, I closed with a line that I think is appropriate for the last words of this book: "I would like to leave you with this…if you should ever find yourself, mentally, spiritually or emotionally down, Get back up! Thank you very much."

1969 SOPHOMORE SEASON

Date	Opponent	Result	Atts	Yds.	Avg.	TD
4-Oct	Missouri	L 17-40	2	1	0.5	0
11-Oct	Purdue	W 31-20	13	50	3.9	0
18-Oct	at Minnesota	W 35-9	31	31	4.9	2
1-Nov	Wisconsin	W 35-7	15	142	9.5	2
8-Nov	Illinois	W 57-0	18	155	8.6	1
15-Nov	at Iowa	W 51-6	21	225	10.7	2
22-Nov	Ohio State	W 24-12	23	84	3.6	0
1-Jan	vs. USC*	L 3-10	18	56	3.1	0
1969 Season Totals			**141**	**864**	**6.1**	**7**

1970 JUNIOR SEASON

Date	Opponent	Result	Atts	Yds.	Avg.	TD
19-Sep	Arizona	W 20-9	18	64	3.6	0
26-Sep	at Washington	W 17-3	17	67	3.9	0
3-Oct	Texas A&M	W 14-10	12	24	2.0	1
10-Oct	at Purdue	W 29-0	22	89	4.0	1
17-Oct	Michigan State	W 34-20	29	129	5.1	3
24-Oct	Minnesota	W 39-13	26	151	5.8	1
31-Oct	at Wisconsin	W 29-15	18	82	4.6	0
7-Nov	Illinois	W 42-0	17	65	3.8	2
14-Nov	Iowa	W 55-0	23	189	8.2	2
21-Nov	at Ohio State	L 9-20	15	31	2.1	0
1970 Season Totals			**197**	**911**	**4.6**	**10**

Billy Taylor Game-by-Game

1971 JUNIOR SEASON

Date	Opponent	Result	Atts	Yds.	Avg.	TD
11-Sep	at Northwestern	W 21-6	28	105	3.8	1
18-Sep	Virginia	W 56-0	15	89	5.9	2
25-Sep	UCLA	W 38-0	25	91	3.6	0
2-Oct	Navy	W 46-0	11	76	6.9	1
9-Oct	at Michigan State	W 24-13	15	117	7.8	2
16-Oct	Illinois	W 35-6	22	103	4.7	1
28-Oct	at Minnesota	W 35-7	33	168	5.0	2
30-Oct	Indiana	W 61-7	11	172	15.6	2
6-Nov	Iowa	W 63-7	15	80	5.3	1
13-Nov	at Purdue	W20-17	17	98	5.8	0
20-Nov	Ohio State	W 10-7	25	118	4.7	1
1-Jan	vs. Stanford*	L 12-13	32	82	2.6	0
1971 Season Totals			**249**	**1297**	**5.2**	**13**
Career Totals			**587**	**3072**	**5.2**	**30**

*Rose Bowl

MICHIGAN CAREER ACCOMPLISHMENTS

➤ Three-time All-American Football Honoree—1969, 1970, 1971
➤ Most Valuable Player, University of Michigan Football—1971
➤ All Big Ten First Team—1969, 1970, 1971
➤ All-time University of Michigan Record Holder—Average Rushing Yards Per Game 102.4 Yards Per Game
➤ Michigan was 26-4 in games Billy Taylor played during his collegiate career

Dr. Billy Taylor Timeline

1949..1954..1966..1967..1968..1969..1970..1971..1972..1975..1977..1980..1981..1992..1997..1998..2001..2003..2004..2005

JANUARY 7, 1949: William Lewis Taylor Jr., is born in Hoxie, Arkansas, on his grandmother's couch. He is the son of William Lewis and Mariah Marie Taylor. This is the third marriage for Mariah Marie Taylor who already has six children by two previous marriages. William Jr. is the only son fathered by William Lewis Taylor.

SPRING 1954: Billy Taylor's father dies of a stroke while working in the sandstone and gravel pits in Memphis, Tennessee. After his death, Mariah Marie moves with her seven children to Barberton, Ohio.

MID-AUGUST 1966: As Billy Taylor prepares for his junior season of football at Barberton High School, Mariah Marie Taylor refuses to sign papers to allow her youngest child to play. She believes football is "too worldly" and she believes he could suffer an injury that would prevent him from getting "a good job" when he is finished with high school.

MID-AUGUST 1967: Mariah Marie Taylor had seen how sad Billy was not playing as a junior and she allows him to play for the Barberton Magics.

SEPTEMBER-NOVEMBER 1967: Fifty-seven different colleges recruit Billy Taylor after he rushes for more than 1,000 yards for Barberton High School. Michigan, Ohio State, Cornell and West Virginia are among his top choices.

JANUARY 27, 1968: Taylor becomes a father for the first time upon the birth of Lewis Askew in Barberton.

FEBRUARY 13, 1968: Billy Taylor confirms to Coach Chalmers "Bump" Elliott that he plans to play football for the University of Michigan. At the time, he is part of the largest African-American recruiting class that Michigan had known. Six other black athletes are signed besides Taylor, including Thom Darden who was also from Ohio. Taylor and Darden would become roommates as freshmen.

OCTOBER 25, 1969: Hampered by a shoulder separation early in his career, Taylor enjoys his first big day as a collegiate player as he rushes for 151 yards and 2 touchdowns in a 35-9 win at Minnesota. He also scores a third touchdown on a pass reception.

NOVEMBER 9, 1969: In the fifth game of his collegiate career, Taylor unleashes an 84-yard touchdown run during a 57-0 trouncing of Illinois.

NOVEMBER 15, 1969: Taylor rushes for a career-best 225 yards, plus two touchdowns, in a 51-6 Michigan rout at Iowa. His close friend Glenn Doughty also runs for 100 yards in this contest.

NOVEMBER 22, 1969: The Wolverines defeat No. 1 ranked Ohio State 24-12 as sophomore Taylor leads all ground gainers with 84 yards on 23 carries. Taylor didn't have a single minus-rushing attempt in this colossal match-up. This victory is considered one of the greatest triumphs in Michigan history.

AUGUST 1, 1970: Taylor and the six other black scholarship players on the Michigan team move into a house on Geddes Road, near Observatory. Taylor, plus Butch Carpenter, Reggie McKenzie, Mike Oldham, Mike Taylor (no relation), Doughty and Darden refer to their new home as "The Den of the Mellow Men."

OCTOBER 17, 1970: Taylor rushes for three touchdowns and 152 yards in the Wolverines 34-20 win against Michigan State.

NOVEMBER 14, 1970: At home against Iowa, Taylor rushes for 189 yards to key a 55-0 triumph.

DECEMBER 17, 1970: Taylor and Michigan teammate Doughty are among a group of college players who travel to Vietnam to entertain the troops. He stays 21 days and is profoundly moved by the experience.

OCTOBER 9-OCTOBER 30, 1971: Over a four-week span in his senior season, Taylor gains 558 yards on 81 carries. That's an average of 6.8 yards per carry. He ran for 117 at Michigan State, 103 at home against Illinois, 168 at Minnesota and finished off his streak with 172 against the Indiana Hoosiers at Michigan Stadium. His 66-yard TD gallop against Indiana was his longest run of the season.

NOVEMBER 7, 1971: Taylor's lone touchdown in a 63-7 rout against Iowa is the 30th of his career. He ties Tom Harmon's school record for career rushing touchdowns.

NOVEMBER 20, 1971: With 2:07 remaining, Taylor uncorks a 21-yard touchdown run to give Michigan a 10-7 win against Ohio State. That run was immortalized because of radio announcer Bob Ufer's dramatic call of the play, punctuated by the passionately yelled "Touchdown Billy Taylor! Touchdown Billy Taylor!" Taylor gains 118 yards in that game, and that touchdown breaks Harmon's career rushing touchdowns' record. It is the 13th 100-yard run of Taylor's Michigan career. One of the Mellow Men, Mike Taylor, makes 14 tackles for Michigan in that contest.

JANUARY 1, 1972: Taylor rushes for 82 yards for Michigan in a heartbreaking 13-12 loss to Stanford in the Rose Bowl. Taylor finishes his collegiate career as Michigan's all-time leading rusher with 3,072 yards. His career average of 102.4 yards per game is a Michigan record that still stands today.

JANUARY 4, 1972: While Taylor is practicing with other top college seniors from around country in preparation for the All-American Bowl, his mother dies suddenly of a heart attack in Barberton.

JANUARY 17, 1972: The City of Barberton hosts "Billy Taylor Day." More than 400 well-wishers gather at the Slovenian Center Hall to honor one of the top athletes in the city's history. There are proclamations from the NAACP, the Fellowship of Christian Athletes, the Ohio House and Senate, plus then-Governor John Gilligan.

FEBRUARY 1, 1972: The Atlanta Falcons select Billy Taylor as the fifth pick in the fifth round—109th overall—in the National Football

League draft. Two of the Mellow Men. Darden (Cleveland) and Mike Taylor (New York Jets), are chosen in the first round, and Reggie McKenzie (Buffalo) is chosen with the first pick in the second round. Doughty (Baltimore) is grabbed 47th overall and Oldham (Washington) is selected in the 10th round.

JUNE 19, 1972: At the invitation of President Richard Nixon, Taylor visits the White House. He receives the invite because he was one of Sport Magazine's College Players of the Month.

JUNE 20, 1972: Taylor's Uncle Eugene, who had consoled Billy upon his mother's death, kills his wife Hattie and then commits suicide in their home in Akron, Ohio. Taylor is in Lubbock, Texas, preparing for a college all-star game when he hears the news. Family members convince him to stay and play in the game.

JUNE 23, 1972: Taylor earns MVP honors after rushing for 92 yards on 17 carries and scoring two touchdowns in the East's 42-20 victory against the West in the 13th annual Coaches All-America Game in Lubbock, Texas.

AUGUST 7, 1972: After getting just four carries in a pre-season game at San Diego, Taylor is waived by the Falcons. The St. Louis Cardinals quickly sign him, but injuries hamper his efforts to make the team. He doesn't play in a regular-season game. He signs with the Calgary Stampeders of the Canadian Football League. Struggling through injuries, he plays three games there before the season is over.

OCTOBER 7, 1972: Taylor tells the *Akron Beacon Journal* that he feels he was a victim of racism in Atlanta's decision to cut him after such a short tryout. He says Atlanta Coach Norm Van Brocklin is a "racist." He says that Van Brocklin was disrespectful of black players. "Speaking for my race, Van Brocklin is setting us back 100 years."

MID-APRIL 1974: The Memphis Southmen of the World Football League signs Taylor to a $25,000 contract. He plays sparingly and eventually ended up with the WFL's Chicago Fire where he had plays in the same backfield with former Cleveland Browns' player Leroy Kelly. Taylor grew up idolizing Kelly.

JANUARY 17, 1975: Minutes after a robbery occurs at the Centran Bank in Barberton, Ohio, Billy Taylor is arrested for driving what police say would have been the get-way car. A police officer shot the robber twice outside the bank. Taylor had not been part of the actual robbery, but he had transported the robber to the bank.

JANUARY 18, 1975: He is formally charged with bank robbery for his role. He hears that if he's convicted, he could face up to 25 years in prison.

JUNE 5, 1975: As a result of a guilty plea, Taylor is sentenced to eight years in prison for his role in the bank robbery. The judge says he can be immediately eligible for parole.

MAY 20, 1977: While still imprisoned in Milan, Michigan, Taylor is awarded his master's degree in adult and continuing education from the University of Michigan. He takes advantage of a work-study program to become the first inmate at Milan to ever earn a graduate degree while incarcerated.

OCTOBER 17, 1977: Taylor is paroled from Milan prison, credited with serving about 30 months of his sentence, counting time spent in the county jail. He immediately accepts a job offer from General Motors.

FEBRUARY 8, 1980: Married shortly after he is released from prison. Taylor and his then-wife become parents of William Lewis Taylor III.

MAY 8, 1981: Taylor's third son is born. He names him Alden James "Butch" Taylor in honor of Butch Carpenter who died a couple of years before while playing pick-up basketball.

JUNE 8, 1992: Taylor and his wife have a daughter and they name her after Taylor's mother, Mariah Marie Taylor. Taylor and his wife eventually divorce after 21 years of marriage.

AUGUST 17, 1997: Homeless and drug and alcohol addicted, Taylor is drinking booze at 5:00 in the morning on the porch of a vacant building when he hears what he strongly believes is the voice of God. By that afternoon, he has sworn off drugs and alcohol and is gainfully employed for the first time in years. He has been clean since that day, without the aid of counseling or any rehabilitation program. "It was a miracle," Taylor says. "That's the only explanation."

OCTOBER 1, 1998: Taylor moves to Las Vegas with the hope of finding a teaching job. He eventually ends up teaching at the Community College of Southern Nevada.

JULY 1, 2001: Taylor is named the Athletic Compliance Officer/Academic Advisor, Department of Athletics at Community College of Southern Nevada.

MAY 17, 2003: Dr. William Taylor receives his Ed.D. in educational leadership from the University of Las Vegas-Nevada. As a young man, Taylor had admired Dr. Martin Luther King and aspired to follow his example by earning his own doctorate.

JULY 1, 2003: Dr. Taylor is named Interim Director, Department of Retention; Retention Coordinator & Academic Advisor at Community College of Southern Nevada.

OCTOBER 4, 2004: Dr. Taylor is inducted into the Summit County Hall of Fame in Akron, Ohio. That night he predicts that he will have his autobiography written and it will be published by the following fall.

APRIL 6, 2005: Author Kevin Allen and Dr. Taylor discuss collaboration on his book. Within three weeks, the duo has a signed an agreement with Immortal Investments Publisher Mike Reddy. The trio agrees that the book would be released in the fall of 2005.

REFLECTIONS

By Dr. Billy Taylor

What About Rhea

To the girl that I met but did not know.
I believe that was four years ago.
I've been told that distance makes the heart grow fonder.
Why we were not in Love I will always wonder?
I received a letter from a friend today.
He told me you have gotten married and moved away.
As I read those words I did not know how to feel.
All I could do was be quiet and sit still.
Four long years you have lingered on my mind.
I stop and wonder what happened to the time?
I knew when I met you that I would not see you for awhile.
And today I'm still waiting even though you have a child.
Often I'll say to myself; I wonder how is Rhea?
When we met it was an unusual circumstance.
You were finally getting free and I was in a trance.
I wonder what's the force behind this mystery.
Is not seeing you again destiny?
Should I write, should I call, should I be happy or blue?
I don't know the answer because I never really knew you.
But, I do know you, that's what my heart keeps telling me.
A man does not always have to touch before he can see.
When I last saw you, you were happy and wore a grin.
And after talking to you I wanted to see what lay within.
You are married now and I pray you are both happy and secure.
For to be with you and make you laugh should be any man's pleasure!
At last, I know what to do about Rhea!
I'll write her tonight, and when I can , I'll go and see her!

By, Bill Taylor
December 22, 1975

Tomorrow

Today finds me still looking forward to tomorrow
And today I am still filled with yesterday's sorrow

There is so much that I would like to express
Maybe tomorrow I will be able to explain this mess

I feel like a man in a foreign land
Who cannot speak the language and have much to understand

I go to bed each night with one thought alone
That when I awake in the morning I will be a day closer to home

Today finds me wondering when will I be free
I do not know the answer but I am sure it is in my destiny

Tomorrow, tomorrow, will you shed some kind of light?
Or will the "good news" come like a thief in the night?

As it nears the time of birth of the son of man
My mind takes me back into time and I long for my homeland

But the spirit of "Him" dwells deep in my soul
So I know that I can bear the suffering until I reach my goal

But I know that one day tomorrow shall actually come my friend
I only pray to God to be able to endure until the end

Some say that tomorrow is too far away for me
Some have eyes but will never be able to see

Feeling vainful today some say that they fear tomorrow
They say that yesterday was no better for the feeling was hollow

This shows a lack of faith and without faith you are lost
I would rather be confined with salvation than free without the cross

I do not fear death, at least not from carnal man
I would fear being without "Him" who could let me live again

Learn to enjoy each day and empty fears of tomorrow
Do not allow yesterday to restrict your life to sorrow

I cannot get home by wishing to be there
But I can endure in my mind by looking unto prayer

Thus, while in the flesh I shall look forward to tomorrow
Therefore, subjecting myself to some human grief and sorrow!

By, Billy Taylor
December 5, 1975

Memphis Tennessee

I couldn't get a drink of water.
I wasn't much older than three.
I couldn't get a drink of water
In Memphis, Tennessee

Into one place and then to another
White people staring and laughing.
So we left quickly, Aunt Emma pulling on me
In Memphis, Tennessee

I was walking and crying
Then, one white woman behind the bar
Held up a cup at her knee for me
In Memphis, Tennessee

My father soon died
And we moved up North you see
But a half a century later I remember 1953
In Memphis, Tennessee

By, William C. Taylor Jr.
January 20, 2003

Freedom

Freedom is walking in the rain for miles.

No early wake up and khaki dress.

And hurryin' to your work detail.

No transactional analysis!

By Bill Taylor
May 28, 1976

Just a Love Affair

Shadows.....
Of people of my past,
Makes me stop and wonder....
If anything is going to last

New friends take the place of images.....
Only tends to remind me,
That there is little to be missed

Changes.... keep occurring all the time
Sometimes sad, sometimes fine

Winter brings the cold yet lovely snow
Springtime warms the heart and makes you glow
Summer greens the grass and clears the sky
Autumn browns the leaves and passes by

Lovers enter in and warm your heart
You deeply miss what wasn't there
But disappointment makes you part
"it" was just a love a fair....

Shadows.....
Of people of my past, makes me stop and wonder....
If "anything" is going to last?

By, Billy Taylor
November 18, 1975

AMERICA IN BLACK AND WHITE

Hello to all the children. What are you going to dream about tonight? How about trying not to see America in Black and White? Adults often say, out of the mouths of babes comes truth and understanding. I wonder if that's still true if you are descendants of slaves. Some smile as they reminisce about their yesterday while some wake up screaming, wishing it was a bad play. Mason and Dixon Line did more than divide America's space—if you dare to close your eyes it shall take you through time from place to place. The "American dream" brought many wealth and put them in places of rule, but there are many who are still waiting for their forty-acres and a mule.

America in Black and White is what I dreamed about last night, so I got up this morning and I began to write.

Memphis, Montgomery, Selma, and Port Chicago put a real colorful stain on America's ego!

America arise, and let all men and women be free! I am talking to America in Black and White. I am talking to you and me—America in Black and White I am talking to you and me! Who knows the original color of the Statue of Liberty? America in Black and White arise and look at me, America in Black and White, color me free! One is never to return a gift, but the Statue of Liberty was sent back, real swift.

I see America in colors, watch me walk and talk. Are you laughing at me? Try to see America in colors before you begin to speak. Arlington lies quiet and it is in Black and White. Close your eyes America, stop seeing in Black and White. We must begin to see in colors and I am telling you this for sure, if we refuse to see in colors, America cannot endure. The Garden of Eden makes a statement about man and his origin – it talks about ribs and bones and not being alone, not the color of man's or woman's skin. Oh America, shame on you! Does anyone try to do what's right? Oh America, when shall we stop seeing in Black and White? Hello to the children, and what are you going to dream about tonight? How about trying to see America in colors, instead of Black and White.

By, Bill Taylor
April 28, 1999

Blessed Unity

Love is heaven, beyond a doubt it is...
so sweet to the taste and soul.
Life becomes ecstasy and living means more...
than to merely exist.

Becoming closer than mother and son...
sharing each other's life and,
growing together as if only one...
God, man and woman.

Beginning at different times...
moving down roads to life,
following a course that twists and winds,
before realizing life's greatest spice.

Believe me when I show you my love...
consider what I say in monotones,
"You are my love-dove"...
love is the essence of my life shown

You were born ripe...
so wonderful, kind and sweet
I mellowed to meet your taste...
I was "sunning", not knowing when we'd meet

Now it is time for the harvest...
overflowing with honey are our fields,
We're careful not to grow them too fast,
so that there will be increases through the years

Standing side by side like pillars...
strong as iron and steel,
we flock like birds of the same feather,
just living, laughing, and living...
throughout timeless years.

By Bill Taylor
July 30, 1976

It's All Over but the Crying

It's all over... but the crying
had a feeling like that,
watching the boys lose the "battle"...
hurt some folks real bad.

It's all over but the crying
it's a shame she left,
cared more about that girl...
than I did for myself.

It's all over...but the crying
that was all of the money I had,
should of have drawn back and let "her whirl"...
May as well have thrown it at a Black-bird.

It's all over but the crying
those beautiful open spaces,
buildings for trees and streets for streams...
Little stays the same.. it seems.

It's all over...but the crying
left home in a real big rush,
bad when you got the "wonderlust"...
Move on down the road.

It's all over but the crying
that big ole' pie in the sky,
mountains, rocks, dust...
Lord says that's all it is to us.

It's all over...but the crying
that ole' eagle with broken wing,
that ole' bumblebee done lost its sting...
That's mean... mean.

It's all over but the crying
if I'd only finished school,
got what I wanted... left the rest.
Tired now.....used to be fresh.

It's all over....but the crying
battle, done left
"her whirl streams against the sky"
broken wing.....rest....then die

By, Billy Taylor— March 19, 1976

Turn Off the Lights

Turn off the lights... Please.
Make the world dark,
So no one can see.

Everything is now for real.
Everyone has to learn to feel.

Is my hair nappy or straight?
Is my skin Black?
Is my skin White?
Can you tell me what time it is?
Now?!.......
Or, is it day?
Is it night?

Whispering, shouting, cursing....
Mostly leads to misery,
Usually because of what we see.

Eye! Heart!....please transplant.
See, with your heart,
Feel, with your eye.

That's right....
Turn off the lights.

By, Bill Taylor
March 12, 1976

A MESSAGE FROM THE PUBLISHER

Michael J. Reddy
Publisher

We are very proud to present Dr. Billy Taylor's extraordinary and inspirational biography. While starring for the University of Michigan Wolverine's football team, B.T., number 42, established his legend as one of the school's greatest football players ever. Co-author Kevin Allen artfully crafts his remarkable life story that demonstrates the depth of obstacles that a courageous and spiritual man can surmount. Taylor's personal and professional struggles, and his ultimate triumph of those relentless hardships, is guaranteed to galvanize and uplift you when you read his truly unbelievable tale. ***Get Back Up and God Bless!***

Immortal Investments Publishing produces timeless books that move, inspire, and spotlight the best of the human spirit manifested by extraordinary human achievement.

Please review and order our other outstanding titles by visiting www.immortalinvestments.com or by calling **1-800-475-2066**.

Please let us know if you have suggestions for other exceptional books or have comments about *Get Back Up*.

***This publishing venture is revolutionary in that the book like all other Immortal Investment titles is not distributed to bookstores. It is available exclusively through Immortal Investments Publishing.

To bring Dr. Billy Taylor to your event for a personal book signing please contact www.immortalinvestments.com.

Order your signed copy by
Dr. Billy Taylor today!
1-800-475-2066.
NOT SOLD IN BOOKSTORES

Immortal Investmants Publishing
35122 W. Michigan Ave. Wayne, MI 48184

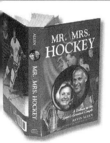

boji books PRESENTS...

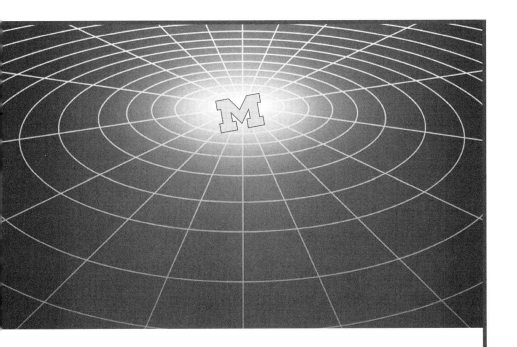